Masters: Blown Glass

DAN DAILEY ■ BRIAN HIRST

■ DANTE MARIONI ■ SUNNY WANG ■

BENJAMIN EDOLS AND KATHY ELLIOTT

■ WILLIAM MORRIS ■ SCOTT CHASELING

■ GABRIELLA BISETTO ■ KAIT RHOADS ■

HIROSHI YAMANO ■ WILLIAM GUDENRATH

■ RICHARD MARQUIS ■ NICK MOUNT ■ PETER HOUK ■

JANE BRUCE ■ WENDY J. FAIRCLOUGH

■ SONJA BLOMDAHL ■ MICHAEL ROGERS ■

BENJAMIN P. MOORE ■ MARK R. MATTHEWS

■ PRESTON SINGLETARY ■ KATHERINE GRAY ■

MAUREEN WILLIAMS ■ BOYD SUGIKI ■

JOSH SIMPSON ■ RICHARD MEITNER

■ DEBORA MOORE ■ MARVIN LIPOFSKY ■

DICK WEISS ■ JOEL PHILIP MYERS

■ JOEY KIRKPATRICK AND FLORA MACE ■

DANIEL SPITZER ■ CAPPY THOMPSON

■ KATHLEEN MULCAHY ■ ROBERT CARLSON ■

LAURA DONEFER ■ WILLIAM BERNSTEIN

■ ROBIN CASS ■ RICHARD ROYAL ■ PAUL MARIONI

Masters: Blown Glass

Major Works by Leading Artists
Curated by Susan Rossi-Wilcox

LARK CRAFTS
A Division of Sterling Publishing Co., Inc.
New York / London

SENIOR EDITOR
Ray Hemachandra

EDITOR
Julie Hale

ART DIRECTOR
Megan Kirby

COVER DESIGNER
Megan Kirby

PRODUCTION
Kay Stafford

CURATOR
Susan Rossi-Wilcox

FRONT COVER, LEFT TO RIGHT:
Benjamin Edols and Kathy Elliott
Leaf, 2003

Dan Dailey
Absent, 1992

Peter Houk
Big Dig #61, 2009

BACK COVER:
Paul Marioni
Whopper Vase, 1997

SPINE:
Sonja Blomdahl
Copper Blue/Aqua, 1998

Library of Congress Cataloging-in-Publication Data

Masters : blown glass : major works by leading artists / [Ray Hemachandra, editor]. -- 1st ed.
    p. cm.
  Includes index.
  ISBN 978-1-60059-474-8 (pb-pbk. with flaps : alk. paper)
  1. Glass art--History--21st century. 2. Blown glass. I. Hemachandra, Ray. II. Title: Blown glass.
  NK5110.5.M37 2010
  748.09'0511--dc22
                              2010000573

10 9 8 7 6 5 4 3 2 1

First Edition

Published by Lark Books, A Division of
Sterling Publishing Co., Inc.
387 Park Avenue South, New York, NY 10016

Text © 2010, Lark Books, a Division of Sterling Publishing Co., Inc.
Photography © 2010, Artist/Photographer

Distributed in Canada by Sterling Publishing,
c/o Canadian Manda Group, 165 Dufferin Street
Toronto, Ontario, Canada M6K 3H6

Distributed in the United Kingdom by GMC Distribution Services,
Castle Place, 166 High Street, Lewes, East Sussex, England BN7 1XU

Distributed in Australia by Capricorn Link (Australia) Pty Ltd.,
P.O. Box 704, Windsor, NSW 2756 Australia

If you have questions or comments about this book, please contact:
Lark Books
67 Broadway
Asheville, NC 28801
828-253-0467

Manufactured in China

ISBN 13: 978-1-60059-474-8

For information about custom editions, special sales, and premium and corporate
purchases, please contact the Sterling Special Sales Department at 800-805-5489 or
specialsales@sterlingpublishing.com.

For information about desk and examination copies available to college and university professors,
requests must be submitted to academic@sterlingpublishing.com. Our complete policy can be
found at www.larkcrafts.com.

Contents

Introduction

WHEN ARTISTS ARE ESPECIALLY GIFTED, their work can provide us with new perspectives on our lives. Through concept, design, and old-fashioned craftsmanship, they illuminate our worldviews and provide us with fresh perceptions of reality. Glassworkers do it all using a medium that's characterized by contradictions.

Sturdy yet fragile, transparent yet luminous, inflexible yet fluid, glass—despite its apparent contrariness—offers a near-limitless degree of creative potential to artists. You'll find ample evidence of this sense of possibility on the pages that follow. Glass is a substance that magically straddles two worlds—art and craft—serving as both an unparalleled medium for the fine arts and a wonderful material for production or decorative work. As a result, in this book you'll find pieces that belong to the decorative genre alongside works that demonstrate deeply conceptual or intellectual ideas.

In this collection, too, you'll discover old and young faces. You'll see artists from around the globe—proof of glass' universal appeal—all of whom take personal approaches to their craft. Some glassworkers ask colleagues to fabricate their forms to ensure that their concepts have the cleanest, sharpest execution possible. Some artists started out blowing glass for others and are now confidently expressing their own ideas. Many artists use glass as a canvas by combining colored elements in the body of a work and

Wendy J. Fairclough
▲ Joy | 2007

etching or painting on the surface. Common to some of the glassblowers in this collection is the practice of using techniques such as casting, flameworking, slumping, and pâte de verre.

Glass functions creatively in many ways. It can serve equally well as a metaphor for fragility or for strength. It can act as either a window or a wall within a work, because it varies in transparency and opacity. In theory, it can be manipulated into any shape or size, be reduced to the thinness of a molecule, or gathered into a magnifying sphere that bends light.

All of these characteristics, which are specific to glass, make it an exciting material with an indomitable and unique spirit. We believe the extraordinary work featured in *Masters: Blown Glass* reflects that spirit. The selected works possess an intellectual rigor and an emotional intensity.

Like an art installation, this book could only have been produced through the generosity of the artists represented and the intelligence and insight reflected in the curator's choices. The wonderful visual magic of glass can be difficult to capture, even in excellent photographs,

Benjamin Edols and Kathy Elliott
▲ **Kamakura Series** | 2002

so we encourage you to visit galleries and museums to see firsthand what makes glass-blown art so special. We hope this book will inspire you to explore the vast and beautiful world of this incredible medium.

Dan Dailey

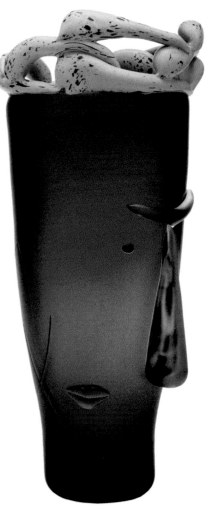

DESIGNED WITH SOPHISTICATION AND CLARITY,
Dan Dailey's beautifully proportioned vases and ingenious sculptural
works reflect a broad creative vision. Working in a style that's clean and
elegant, and using colors that are gloriously rich, Dailey combines glass,
metals, and other materials in ways that optimize the overall effect of a
piece. Dailey often uses human or animal figures as decorative elements
on his vases, posing them in ways that suggest motion and rhythm.
Other pieces demonstrate his envisioning of music. These complexly
designed sculptural collages represent the feeling of the sounds that
come from various instruments.

   Regardless of subject matter or intention, the mood and attitude of
Dailey's pieces are always supported by his choice of color and form.
The New Hampshire-based artist has participated in more than 300
invitational exhibits and has had numerous one-person shows, including
a major retrospective at the Renwick Gallery of the Smithsonian
American Art Museum in Washington, D.C.

Pretenders | 2008 ▶
25 x 14½ x 9 inches
(63.5 x 36.8 x 22.9 cm)
Blown glass, nickel- and gold-
plated bronze, patina; sandblasted,
acid polished, fabricated
Photo by Bill Truslow

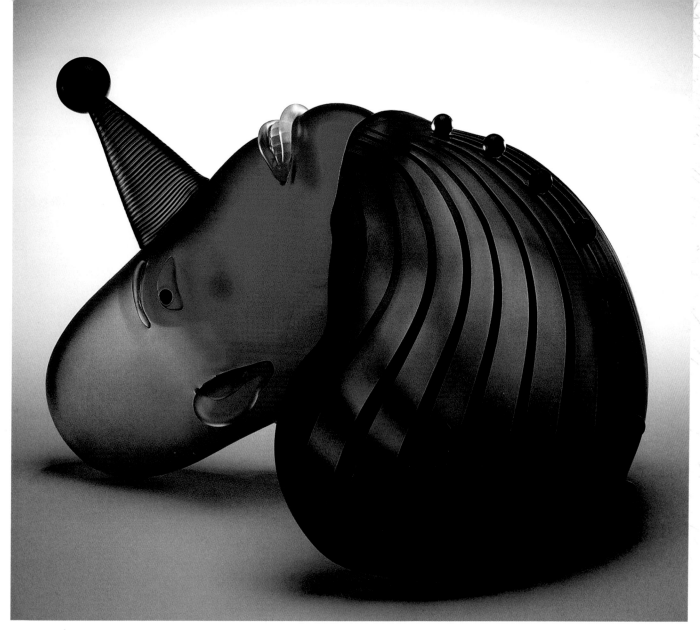

▲ **Fool** | 2004

12 x 18½ x 15½ inches (30.5 x 47 x 39.4 cm)
Blown glass; sandblasted, acid-polished

Photo by Bill Truslow

◀ **Tollbooth and Hitchhiker** │ 1983

11 x 6½ x 4 inches (27.9 x 16.5 x 10.2 cm)
Blown crystal; sandblasted, acid-polished

Photo by Bill Truslow

Talls and Vents │ 1981 ▶

12 x 7½ x 7½ inches (30.5 x 19.1 x 19.1 cm)
Blown glass; cast, sandblasted, acid-polished

Photo by Bill Truslow

"Although my work features a variety of shapes, I see the pieces as offshoots of classic forms."

◀ **Hot Wind** | 1984

11 x 8½ x 8½ inches
(27.9 x 21.6 x 21.6 cm)
Blown glass; sandblasted,
acid-polished

Photo by Bill Truslow

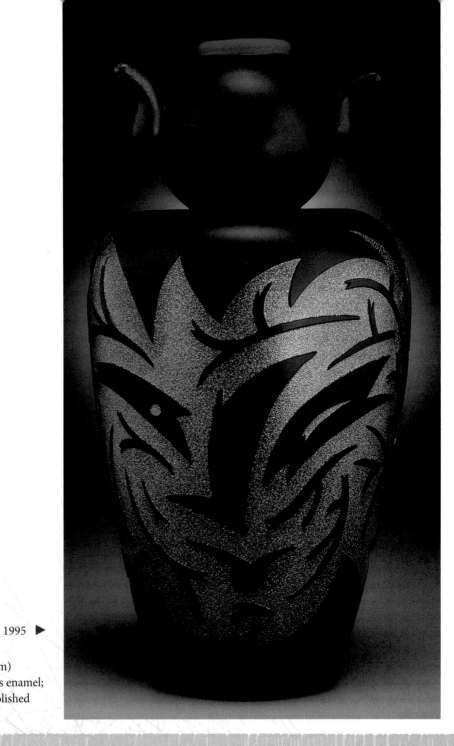

"When I began applying human facial features to vessels, I found that some of the pieces resembled busts. The sense of formal portraiture the bust offered, along with the potential for figurative realism, really appealed to me and opened up new possibilities for my work."

Poison Ivy Man | 1995 ▶

22 x 12 x 12 inches
(55.9 x 30.5 x 30.5 cm)
Blown glass, vitreous enamel;
sandblasted, acid-polished

Photo by Bill Truslow

◀ **New York–4** │ 1993

20 x 12 x 12 inches (50.8 x 30.5 x 30.5 cm)
Blown glass; sandblasted, acid-polished
Photo by Bill Truslow

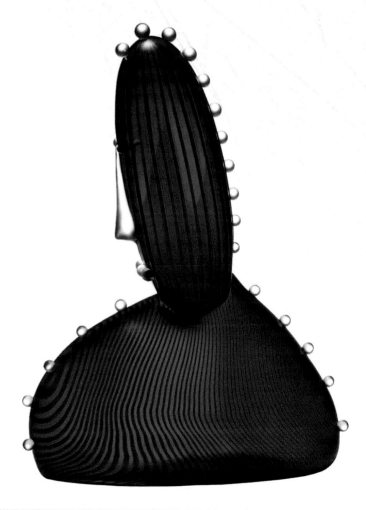

Repose │ 2004 ▶

22½ x 17½ x 8 inches (57.2 x 44.5 x 20.3 cm)
Blown glass, nickel-plated bronze, patina;
sandblasted, acid-polished, fabricated
Photo by Bill Truslow

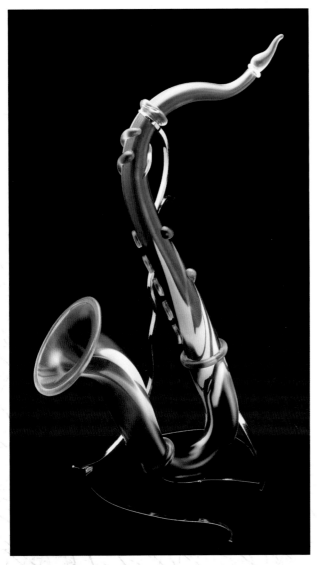

▲ Synthesis | 2002

28 x 13 x 20 inches (71.1 x 33 x 50.8 cm)
Blown glass, nickel-plated bronze, patina;
sandblasted, acid-polished, fabricated

Photo by Bill Truslow

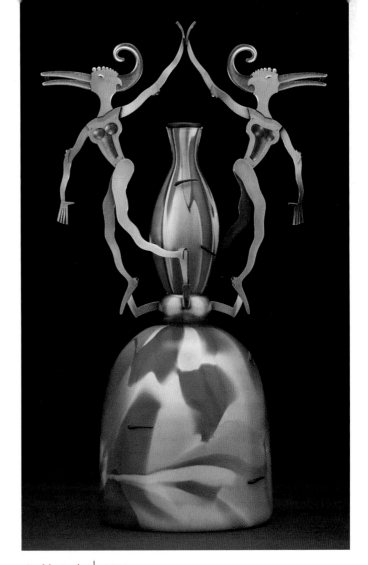

▲ Absent | 1992

23 x 11 x 11 inches (58.4 x 27.9 x 27.9 cm)
Blown glass; sandblasted, acid-polished

Photo by Bill Truslow

"Using figures as the decorative elements of a vase, taking the place of handles in some cases, provides a symmetry to the piece that relates it to a long line of formal tradition."

◀ **Passion** | 2003

56 x 26 x 15 inches (142.2 x 66 x 38.1 cm)
Blown glass, nickel- and gold-plated bronze, patina;
sandblasted, acid-polished, fabricated
Photos by Bill Truslow

Brian Hirst

EXPLORING IN HIS LATEST COLLECTION A CONCEPT that he calls "shadow guardians," Australian artist Brian Hirst works with three-dimensional vessels to create pieces that appear nearly two-dimensional. The remarkable contrast between perspectives makes the viewer keenly aware of their similarities and differences; each dimension enhances the appeal of the other. In some works Hirst pairs a cast glass vessel with a steel panel that's engraved with a rendering of the vessel itself, and the effect is like getting a privileged peek at an artist's drawing or an architect's sketch—we witness form and structure firsthand, with their attendant nuances of shade and texture.

Hirst favors shapes reminiscent of ancient ritual vessels and uses a silvering surface treatment that mimics metal. Carefully cold-worked details give a decorative quality to his pieces, suggesting ethnicity and preciousness. There's something especially beguiling about Hirst's brilliant work, which brings to mind excavated Chinese bronzes. His vessels and bowls are in collections around the world, including the Corning Museum of Glass in Corning, New York, and the Museum of Modern Art in Kyoto, Japan.

Shadow Offering Bowl | 2007 ▶

19¹¹⁄₁₆ x 23³⁄₁₆ x 20¹⁄₁₆ inches
(50 x 59 x 51 cm)
Blown glass, platinum, enamel,
stainless steel; cast, engraved
Photo by Michael Myers

▲ **Shadow Guardian** | 2008

16⅛ x 23³⁄₁₆ x 11¹³⁄₁₆ inches (41 x 59 x 30 cm)

Blown glass, platinum, stainless steel, enamel; cast, engraved

Photo by Greg Piper

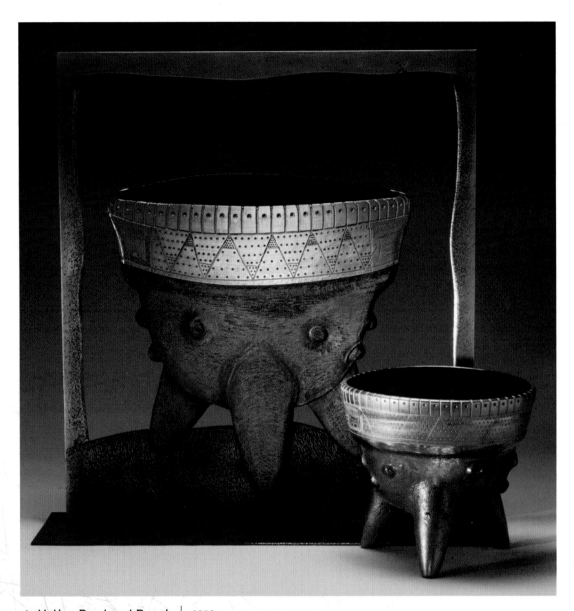

▲ Votive Bowl and Panel | 2002

39¾ x 39⅜ x 23⅝ inches (101 x 100 x 60 cm)

Blown glass, platinum, stainless steel; cast, engraved

Photo by Greg Piper

"I'm very interested in vessels and their history, in how they're used and valued as objects. My own practice has been influenced by homewares from Scandinavia and Japan—by the aesthetics and philosophies that underpin them."

◀ **Offering Bowl III** │ 2002

$11^{13}/_{16}$ x $14^{3}/_{16}$ x $14^{3}/_{16}$ inches
(30 x 36 x 36 cm)
Blown glass, platinum;
cast, engraved

Photo by Greg Piper

"I find the juxtaposition of two- and three-dimensional renderings of the same idea appealing because it suggests an object and its shadow, a being and its alter ego.**"**

Guardian and Image | 2007 ▶

24 x 23⅝ x 9¹³⁄₁₆ inches
(61 x 60 x 25 cm)
Blown glass, platinum,
sheet glass, stainless steel,
enamels; cast, engraved
Photo by Michael Myers

◀ **Shadow Guardian Form** | 2007

15⁵⁄₁₆ x 18⅛ x 7⅞ inches
(38 x 46 x 20 cm)
Blown glass, platinum, stainless steel,
enamel; cast, engraved

Photo by Michael Myers

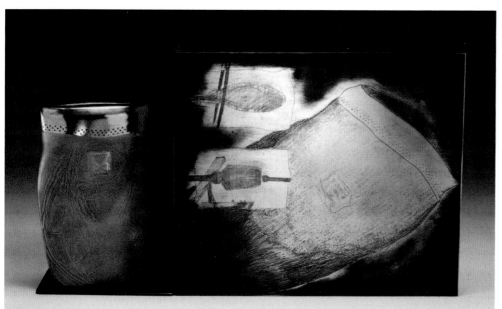

◀ **Guardian III and Images** | 2002

19¹¹⁄₁₆ x 35⁷⁄₁₆ x 7⅞ inches
(50 x 90 x 20 cm)
Blown glass, platinum, enamel,
stainless steel; cast, engraved

Photo by Greg Piper

BRIAN HIRST

Shadow Votive Bowl I | 2004 ▶

19¼ x 27⅛ x 25⁹⁄₁₆ inches
(49 x 69 x 65 cm)
Blown glass, platinum, enamel,
stainless steel; cast, engraved

Photo by Greg Piper

◀ Votive Bowl and Shadow | 2002

11¹³⁄₁₆ x 14¹⁵⁄₁₆ x 14³⁄₁₆ inches
(30 x 38 x 36 cm)
Blown glass, platinum,
stainless steel, enamel;
cast, engraved

Photo by Greg Piper

"The use of silver, white gold, and copper foils that I roll onto the layers of hot glass while blowing a vessel emphasizes its surface. The foils contrast with each other in a central motif like a small print—an influence taken from my many years of printmaking."

▲ **Scarlet Votive Bowl** │ 2007

13¾ x 16¹⁵⁄₁₆ x 16⅛ inches
(35 x 43 x 41 cm)
Blown glass, platinum, enamel;
cast, engraved
Photo by Michael Myers

Shadow Offering Bowl │ 2007 ▶

14¹⁵⁄₁₆ x 23³⁄₁₆ x 20¹⁄₁₆ inches
(38 x 59 x 51 cm)
Blown glass, platinum, enamel,
stainless steel; cast, engraved
Photo by Michael Myers

BRIAN HIRST

Dante Marioni

COMBINING SLEEK VENETIAN STYLISHNESS with uninhibited American exuberance, Dante Marioni has an aesthetic that's all his own. The son of Paul Marioni, Dante was introduced to glasswork at a young age, acquiring the skills that now allow him to express a very personal contemporary vision. At once whimsical and classical, playful and elegant, his pieces possess voluptuousness and an unreserved charm. Referencing ancient Greek and Italian vessel designs, Marioni lengthens and exaggerates traditional shapes. He works on a large scale, often creating pieces that are nearly five feet (1.5 m) tall.

Alone, Marioni's vessels are sublime and seductive; arranged in groups, they're transformed from traditional icons into dramatic ensembles that showcase his skill and instinct for imaginative design. With their elongated lines and surprising proportions, Marioni's vases and urns have a sculptural quality. Based in Washington, Marioni has received numerous awards, including honors from the Louis Comfort Tiffany Foundation and the Museum of Arts and Design in New York City. His work is in museums and galleries around the world.

Red with Yellow Mosaic Vase | 2001 ▶
34 x 8 x 8 inches (86.4 x 20.3 x 20.3 cm)
Blown glass
Photo by Russell Johnson

◀ **Blue and Green Leaves** | 2009

Tallest: 38 inches (96.5 cm)
Blown glass

Photo by Russell Johnson

Vessel Display Clear with Black | 2006 ▶

54 x 26 x 5 inches (137.2 x 66 x 12.7 cm)

Blown glass, wood

Photos by Russell Johnson

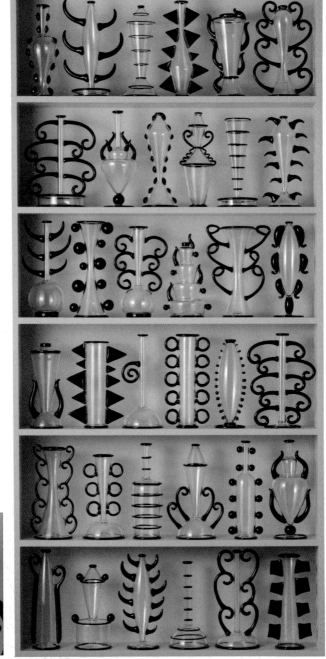

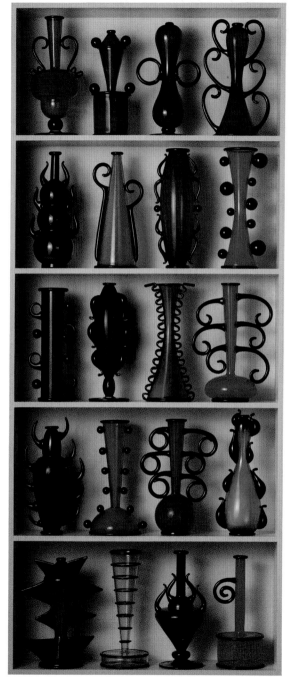

"As a glassblower, I find that creating a form is the real challenge. Color is the easy part."

▲ **Leaves Black with Red and Blue** | 2007

Tallest: 21 inches (53.3 cm)
Blown glass
Photo by Russell Johnson

◀ **Colored Vessel Display** | 2007

45 x 19 x 5 inches (114.3 x 48.3 x 12.7 cm)
Blown glass, wood
Photo by Russell Johnson

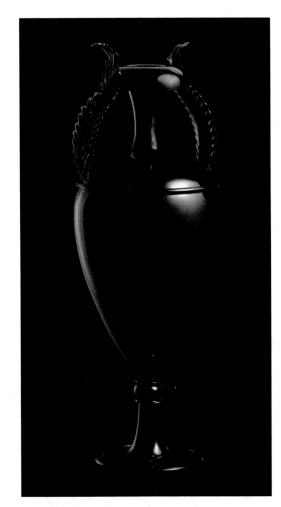

▲ **Black Urn** | 2007

28 x 11 inches (71.1 x 27.9 cm)
Blown glass

Photo by Russell Johnson

Black and White Reticello Vases | 2007 ▶

Tallest: 38 inches (96.5 cm)
Blown glass

Photo by Russell Johnson

"I tend to work on one object at a time and focus my energy on learning how to make a particular piece before moving to the next one."

◄ **Poppy** | 2007
18 x 12 x 12 inches
(45.7 x 30.5 x 30.5 cm)
Blown glass
Photo by Russell Johnson

44 x 13 x 13 inches (111.8 x 33 x 33 cm)
Blown glass

Photo by Russell Johnson

▲ **Gambo Vases, Black and White** | 2000

Each: 44 inches (111.8 cm) tall
Blown glass

Photo by Russell Johnson

DANTE MARIONI

"When I started blowing glass, I discovered that I liked tall, thin forms. When I make preliminary drawings for pieces, that's the way they come out—tall and thin. It can take me several years to make what I've drawn."

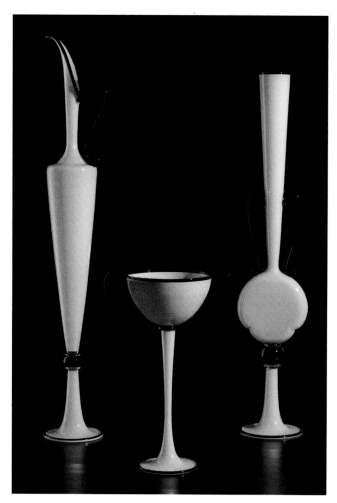

▲ Ivory Trio | 2007
Tallest: 40 inches (101.6 cm)
Blown glass
Photo by Russell Johnson

▲ Green Reticello Leaf and Purple Acorn | 2007
Acorn: 10 x 15 inches (25.4 x 38.1 cm)
Leaf: 27 x 12 x 8 inches (68.5 x 30.4 x 20.3 cm)
Blown glass
Photo by Russell Johnson

Sunny Wang

WITH VESSELS AND SCULPTURES THAT FOCUS on the origins and essence of human life, Taiwanese artist Sunny Wang displays her expertise in a range of different styles—a mastery of diverse forms that makes her work hard to categorize. Her cell-inspired pieces feature a bubble shape, which to Wang symbolizes the open, receptive atmosphere that exists when creative ideas are conceived. Other pieces draw on the complexity, beauty, and individuality of Chinese calligraphy characters, icons that have a strong personal and philosophical resonance for the artist. She etches these characters onto simply designed glass forms, playing up the linear beauty of each symbol. The calligraphy characters in turn emphasize the polished quality of the glass and the light that permeates it.

Wang encourages viewers to touch her pieces, as if they were touching a simple truth or a crystallized moment of happiness. Based in Hong Kong, China, she has participated in exhibitions around the world. Her works are represented in public and private collections in Italy, France, Germany, Sweden, and the United States.

Ru Ru | 2009 ▶
Largest: 13 x 6⁵⁄₁₆ x 6⁵⁄₁₆ inches
(33 x 16 x 16 cm)
Blown glass; sandblasted,
engraved
Photo by artist

10⅝ x 9¹/₁₆ x 7⁷/₁₆ inches
(27 x 23 x 19 cm)
Blown glass; cut, hand finished
Photo by Michal Kluvanek

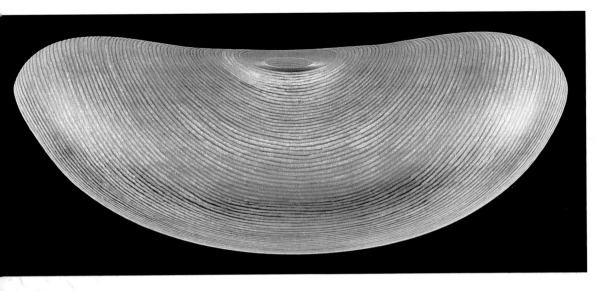

◀ **Fingerprint Cell** | 2000
$4^{5}/_{16}$ x $8^{1}/_{4}$ x $8^{1}/_{4}$ inches
(11 x 21 x 21 cm)
Blown glass; cut, engraved,
hand finished
Photos by artist

"In my work I try to transfer not only the literal qualities of Chinese calligraphy characters but also the emotive qualities that calligraphy arouses."

Clear Cell | 1998 ▶
$6^{11}/_{16}$ x $9^{1}/_{16}$ x $9^{1}/_{16}$ inches
(17 x 23 x 23 cm)
Blown glass; cut
Photo by artist

SUNNY WANG

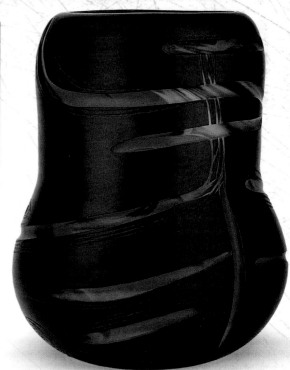

Good Salary/Prosperity | 2001 ▶

10⅝ x 8⅝ x 5⅞ inches (27 x 22 x 15 cm)
Blown glass; sandblasted, engraved,
hand finished

Photos by artist

◀ Green Longevity | 2000

10⅝ x 7¹/₁₆ x 4¹¹/₁₆ inches (27 x 18 x 12 cm)
Blown glass; cut, sandblasted,
engraved, hand finished

Photos by artist

SUNNY WANG

"In my work, the legibility of the calligraphy characters isn't the focus.

Instead, I seek to present a symbolic image that viewers will appreciate.**"**

Red Longevity │ 2001 ▶

10¼ x 7¹⁄₁₆ x 5⅛ inches
(26 x 18 x 13 cm)
Blown glass; sandblasted,
engraved, hand finished

Photos by artist

▼ Luck and Good Salary │ 2001

11 x 7$\frac{1}{16}$ x 5$\frac{11}{16}$ inches
(28 x 18 x 14.5 cm)
Blown glass, enamel; sandblasted,
engraved, hand finished

Photo by artist

▲ Happy │ 2001

11 x 8$\frac{5}{8}$ x 6$\frac{11}{16}$ inches
(28 x 22 x 17 cm)
Blown glass; sandblasted,
engraved, hand finished

Photo by artist

◀ **Golden Longevity** | 2001

8⅝ x 10¼ x 5⅞ inches
(22 x 26 x 15 cm)
Blown glass; sandblasted,
engraved, hand finished

Photos by artist

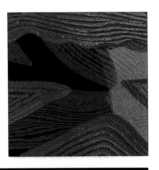

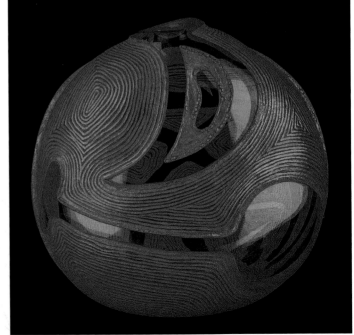

Home and Full Moon | 2000 ▶

9¹⁄₁₆ x 8⅝ x 4⁵⁄₁₆ inches
(23 x 22 x 11 cm)
Blown glass; sandblasted,
engraved, hand finished

Photos by artist

"I like making forms that appear three dimensional, because light passes naturally through them. Viewers get to witness a dialogue between glass and light."

◄ **Spring Longevity** | 2006
$9\frac{13}{16}$ x $5\frac{1}{2}$ x $4\frac{11}{16}$ inches
(25 x 14 x 12 cm)
Blown glass; sandblasted,
engraved, hand finished
Photo by Michal Kluvanek

Benjamin Edols & Kathy Elliott

FEATURING LUSH, SPIRITED COLORS and wonderfully sensual forms, the sculptures of Kathy Elliott and Ben Edols are lavish and captivating. He incorporates Venetian glass techniques and classical shapes into the work, while she heightens the physicality of each form by adding embellishments. In their fluidly designed, plant-inspired pieces, the curvaceous lines of leaves, seeds, and other natural parts are exaggerated in a lively, candid way, giving each work a pronounced organic quality. Cut systematically around a piece, Elliott's harmonious, cold-worked lines impart details that remind the viewer of a well-tended Japanese meditation garden.

Native Australians, Elliott and Edols are inspired by the continent's unique botanical shapes and architecture. Their vessels transport us to places that seem familiar and yet are extraordinary. Elliott and Edols have been collaborating since 1993 and are based in Sydney. Their work has been exhibited in Australia, Japan, the United States, Germany, England, and Italy.

Kamakura Series | 2002 ▶
Tallest: 29⅛ inches (74 cm)
Blown glass; wheel cut
Photo by Greg Piper

▲ **Capillary Reclining Leaf** | 2009

8¼ x 33⁷⁄₁₆ x 13¾ inches (21 x 85 x 35 cm)

Glass; hot formed, wheel cut

Photo by Torunn Momtazi

▲ **Unraveled Sphere** | 1997

10¼ x 10¼ x 10¼ inches
(26 x 26 x 26 cm)
Blown glass; wheel cut

Photo by Ian Hobbs

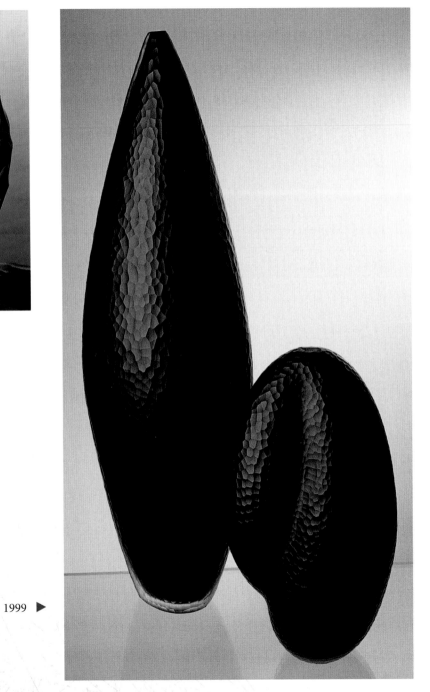

Ebony Flank, Ebony Crease | 1999 ▶

Flank: 25³⁄₁₆ inches (64 cm) tall
Crease: 12⁹⁄₁₆ inches (32 cm) tall
Blown glass; wheel cut

Photo by Peter Scott

◀ **Leaf** │ 2003

20⅞ x 10⅝ x 4⁵⁄₁₆ inches
(53 x 27 x 11 cm)
Blown glass; wheel cut
Photo by Greg Piper

*"Glass is a medium
that allows us
to explore color
and light,
as well as form."*

"We try to make sculptural forms that have tension and rhythm.

We also try to exploit the wonderful qualities of glass."

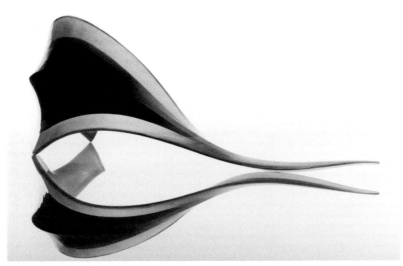

▲ **Window Series: Reclining Leaf** | 2009

7⅞ x 34¼ x 12⁹⁄₁₆ inches (20 x 87 x 32 cm)
Glass; hot formed, wheel cut

Photo by Greg Piper

Reclining Leaf | 2007 ▶

5½ x 34⅗ x 11¹³⁄₁₆ inches
(14 x 88 x 30 cm)
Glass; hot-formed, wheel cut

Photo by Greg Piper

◀ **Bud, Stem, Leaf** | 2007
Tallest: 24⅜ inches (62 cm)
Blown glass; wheel cut
Photo by Greg Piper

"A sense of discipline in the studio is important to us, but we balance it with progression and experimentation."

▲ **Curled Leaf** | 2004

24 x 21⅝ x 4¹¹⁄₁₆ inches
(61 x 55 x 12 cm)
Glass; hot formed, wheel cut
Photo by Greg Piper

Furrow | 2002 ▶

29¹⁵⁄₁₆ x 5½ x 5½ inches
(76 x 14 x 14 cm)
Blown glass; wheel cut
Photo by Greg Piper

Sway Series | 2008 ▶

Waratah: 13 x 10¼ x 10¼ inches
(33 x 26 x 26 cm)
Bottle: 34⅝ x 7⁷⁄₁₆ x 7⁷⁄₁₆ inches
(88 x 19 x 19 cm)
Blown glass; wheel cut
Photo by Greg Piper

◀ **Groove II** | 1998

28 x 5⅞ x 5⅞ inches
(71 x 15 x 15 cm)
Blown glass; wheel cut
Photo by Peter Scott

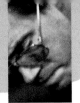

William Morris

FEW ARTISTS HAVE THE TALENT REQUIRED to take iconographic forms and make them their own. William Morris succeeds beautifully at this feat with his distinctive interpretations of ancient symbols and relics. His work is big, colorful, and psychologically imposing, and it has a strong ethnic heart. Morris gathers much of his inspiration from ancient Egyptian, Asian, and Native American cultures, yet his art is culturally distinct, embodying a spiritual quality that contrasts old beliefs with those of the modern world.

Morris often references prehistoric wall paintings. As a result, his work awakens a primordial pull in the viewer—a fresh awareness of nature and an urgent sense of spirituality. Morris favors earth tones, but when he uses color, especially red, it's so well grounded within the composition that it serves as an accent, rather than intruding on the overall harmony of the piece. Cleanly made, elegant in form, and intriguing in its commentary on civilization, his revelatory work brings to mind the character, as well as the trappings, of a culture that might have existed in a different era. Morris, who lives in Washington state, has received many honors, including awards from the Smithsonian Institution and the American Craft Council.

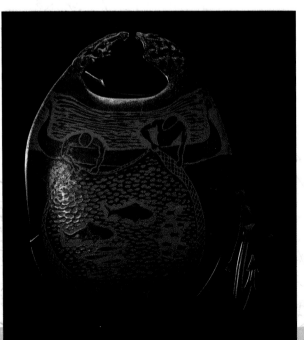

◀ **Fish Trap** | 2007
17 x 9 x 5 inches (43.2 x 22.9 x 12.7 cm)
Blown glass, steel stand
Photo by Rob Vinnedge

▲ **Medicine Jar** | 2006

    32 x 9 x 9 inches (81.3 x 22.9 x 22.9 cm)

    Blown glass

    Photo by Rob Vinnedge

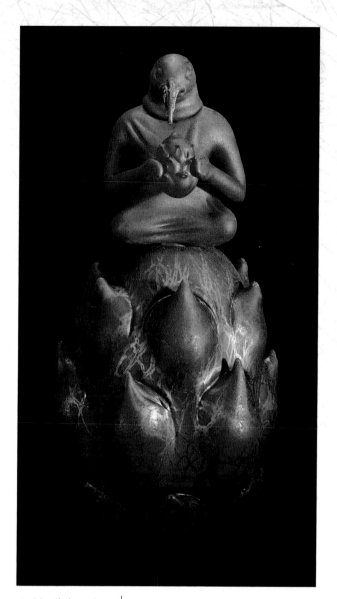

▲ **Medicine Jar** | 2006

    15 x 6 x 6 inches (38.1 x 15.2 x 15.2 cm)

    Blown glass

    Photo by Rob Vinnedge

▲ **Fish Trap** | 2007

17 x 14 x 6 inches (43.2 x 35.6 x 15.2 cm)

Blown glass

Photo by Rob Vinnedge

▲ **Suspended Artifact** | 1995

28 x 28 x 7 inches (71.1 x 71.1 x 17.8 cm)
Blown glass, steel stand
Photo by Rob Vinnedge

▲ **Suspended Artifact** | 1996

32 x 25 x 5 inches
(81.3 x 63.5 x 12.7 cm)
Blown glass, steel stand
Photo by Rob Vinnedge

"The glassblowing process is very humbling. I've always been appreciative of how much I'm able to get away with."

WILLIAM MORRIS

"Glassblowing is the closest thing
to alchemy that I know."

▲ **Horse Rattle** | 1997

21 x 23 x 5 inches (53.3 x 58.4 x 12.7 cm)
Blown glass, steel stand
Photo by Rob Vinnedge

▲ **Rhyton Vessel** | 1997

21 x 23 x 7 inches (53.3 x 58.4 x 17.8 cm)
Blown glass, steel stand
Photo by Rob Vinnedge

▲ Ravens on Urn ｜ 1999

    18 x 18 x 16 inches (45.7 x 45.7 x 40.6 cm)

    Blown glass

    Photo by Rob Vinnedge

◄ Mazorca | 2004
Largest: 11 x 33 x 5 inches
(27.9 x 83.8 x 12.7 cm)
Blown glass
Photo by Rob Vinnedge

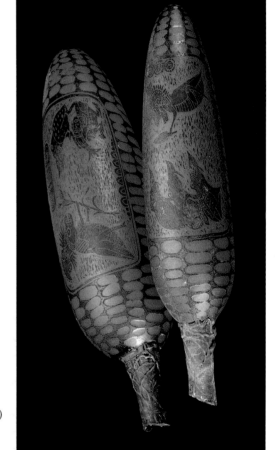

"Although my work is shaped by contemporary life
and technology, it contemplates fragments from the
past, reinventing the stories and rituals that live on
in ancient artifacts."

Mazorca | 2004 ►
Largest: 10 x 32 x 8 inches (25.4 x 81.3 x 20.3 cm)
Blown glass, steel stand
Photo by Rob Vinnedge

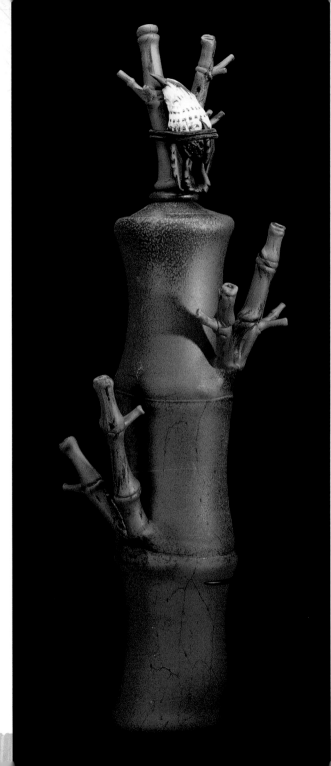

Medicine Jar | 2006 ▶

32 x 9 x 9 inches
(81.3 x 22.9 x 22.9 cm)
Blown glass

Photos by Rob Vinnedge

Scott Chaseling

WHIMSICALLY SHAPED WORKS ENLIVENED BY VIBRANT illustrations, Scott Chaseling's vessels reflect his wit, intelligence, and sense of the surreal. Painted, fused, blown, and ground, his pieces feature vignettes of personal narratives—remarkable, dreamlike moments rendered in colors that are nearly psychedelic. Chaseling's illustrations frequently depict male figures who seem to be caught in fantastic situations or are humbled by circumstance. His paintings often encircle each vessel, and he uses this circular motif, which has been prevalent in his work for many years, as a reference to the idea of completeness or perfection.

With a clear appreciation for the absurd, Chaseling creates remarkably detailed vases and vessels that powerfully communicate a range of moods and emotions. Based in Berlin, Germany, Chaseling has participated in exhibits throughout Europe, Japan, and the United States.

Waiting Time | 2004 ▶

$11^{13}/_{16}$ x $4^{11}/_{16}$ x $4^{11}/_{16}$ inches (30 x 12 x 12 cm)
Blown glass; painted, fused, carved, acid-etched
Photo by artist

◀ **Suspended Heaven** | 2008
23⅝ x 8⅝ x 8⅝ inches (60 x 22 x 22 cm)
Blown glass; sand blasted, acid-etched
Photo by Richard Walker

"The figure is always the focal point in my work. Through form or through imagery, the body tells the story.**"**

▲ **Change of Gears** | 2005
13⅜ x 7⅞ x 7⅞ inches (34 x 20 x 20 cm)
Blown glass; painted, fused, carved, acid-etched
Photo by Rob Little

▲ **The Passing** | 2005
22¹³⁄₁₆ x 8¼ x 8¼ inches (58 x 21 x 21 cm)
Blown glass; painted, fused, carved, acid-etched
Photo by Rob Little

What Goes Around | 2005 ▶

25³⁄₁₆ x 9¹⁄₁₆ x 9¹⁄₁₆ inches
(64 x 23 x 23 cm)
Blown glass; painted, fused,
carved, acid-etched

Photos by Rob Little

◀ When Will It Stop | 2005

9¹³⁄₁₆ x 7⁷⁄₁₆ x 7⁷⁄₁₆ inches
(25 x 19 x 19 cm)
Blown glass; painted, fused,
carved, acid-etched

Photos by Rob Little

22⁷⁄₁₆ x 9¹⁄₁₆ x 9¹⁄₁₆ inches (57 x 23 x 23 cm)
Blown glass; painted, fused, carved, acid-etched
Photos by Rob Little

"The glass process comes as a respite to painting. Although more time consuming and risky, glassblowing relieves the demands of the imagery."

▲ Home Comforts | 2005
22¹³⁄₁₆ x 7¹⁄₁₆ x 7¹⁄₁₆ inches (58 x 18 x 18 cm)
Blown glass; painted, fused, carved, acid-etched
Photos by Rob Little

SCOTT CHASELING

◀ **Time Line** │ 2005

21¼ x 8⅝ x 8⅝ inches
(54 x 22 x 22 cm)
Blown glass; painted, fused,
carved, acid-etched

Photos by Rob Little

Like a Second Home │ 2005 ▶

20⅞ x 7⁷⁄₁₆ x 7⁷⁄₁₆ inches
(53 x 19 x 19 cm)
Blown glass; painted, fused,
carved, acid-etched

Photo by Rob Little

"The paintings in my glass pieces are frames of a continuum—segments of stories or pages from a journal. They're framed by glass through fusing and blowing."

▲ **Wings over Words** | 2008

23⅝ x 8⅝ x 8⅝ inches
(60 x 22 x 22 cm)
Blown glass; sand blasted,
acid-etched

Photos by Richard Walker

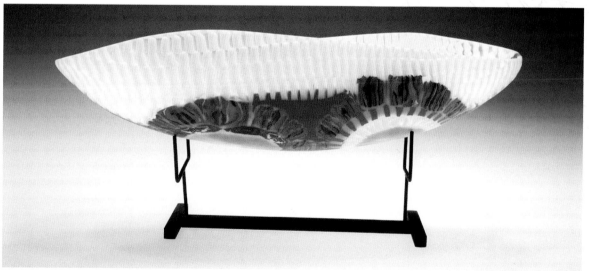

▲ **Last Salt** | 2004

7¹⁄₁₆ x 11 x 5⅛ inches (18 x 28 x 13 cm)

Blown glass, metal; painted, fused, carved, acid-etched

Photos by Rob Little

Gabriella Bisetto

GLASSBLOWERS ARE NECESSARILY INTERESTED IN BREATH CONTROL, but Gabriella Bisetto finds particular relevance in the quantity of air a single individual may dispatch. This phenomenon serves as one of her main inspirations, and she often explores it in her work. Two of her series, *Shape of Breath* and *One Deep Breath*, delve into this ongoing curiosity and feature pieces that are delicate and supple. Other works survey concepts related to man's physicality in very direct ways, by illustrating the water ratio of the human body or using blood-filled scientific glassware—choices that have resulted in some of her most powerful pieces.

Often thin-walled and fluid, Bisetto's glass sculptures have an ephemeral, bubble-like quality that adds to the illusion she creates—that of registering the activities of the human body as it functions from day to day. Thanks to their emphasis on the corporeal, Bisetto's works serve as profound symbols of mortality. As she focuses on measuring, understanding, and translating humanity's physical existence through blown glass and hot sculpting, Bisetto creates provocative, unforgettable work. Based in Adelaide, Australia, Bisetto exhibits regularly throughout Europe and the United States.

▼ **Holding My Breath** | 2007
Largest block: 4¹¹⁄₁₆ x 3⁹⁄₁₆ x 1⁹⁄₁₆ inches (12 x 9 x 4 cm)
Hot glass, breath
Photo by Grant Hancock

▲ **One Deep Breath** │ 2006

9⁷⁄₁₆ x 13¾ x 7⅞ inches (24 x 35 x 20 cm)
Blown glass, stainless steel base

Photo by Michael Haines

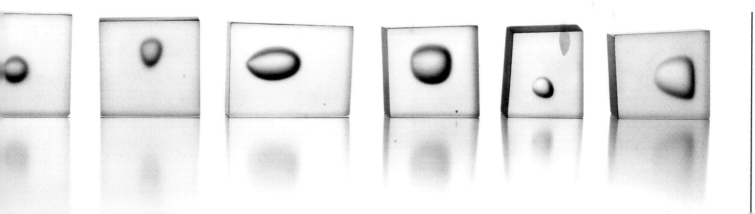

▲ **The Shape of Breath #1** | 2007

15¾ x 15¾ x 11¹³⁄₁₆ inches (40 x 40 x 30 cm)
Blown glass, stainless steel base; hand polished

Photo by Grant Hancock

11¹³⁄₁₆ x 11¹³⁄₁₆ x 11¹³⁄₁₆ inches (30 x 30 x 30 cm)
Blown glass; cut, hand polished

Photo by Michael Harris

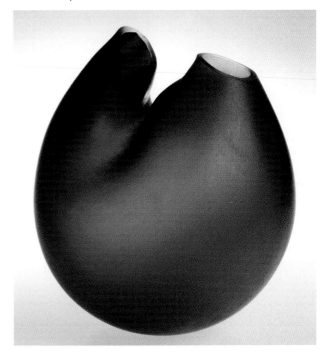

▼ **Crease** | 2005

8⅝ x 8⅝ x 19¹¹⁄₁₆ inches (22 x 22 x 50 cm)
Blown glass; hand polished

Photo by Michael Haines

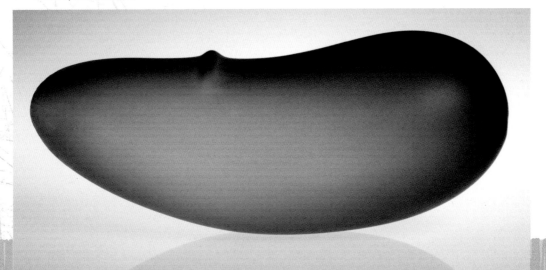

GABRIELLA PISETTO

"I was seeking a new method for conveying my ideas of the body more succinctly through glassblowing when I made a work that measured the volume of my lungs by simply exhaling one big breath into a small amount of glass on the end of the blowpipe. The process took only as long as it took me to exhale, and the ethereal bubble that resulted—a visible measure of my breath—transformed the way I approached glass as a material."

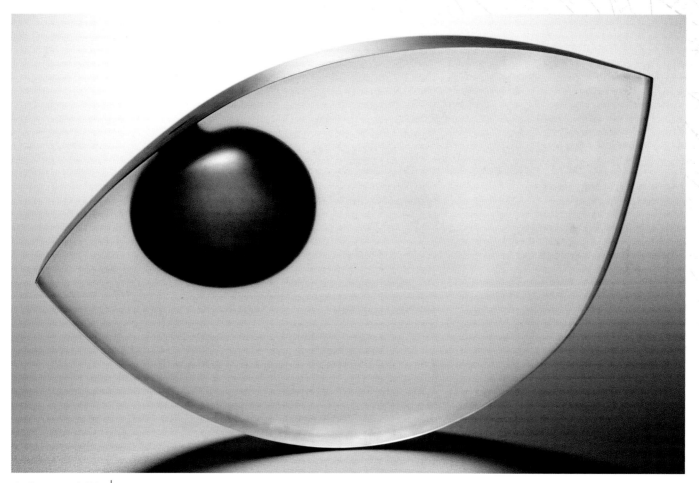

▲ **Segment #1** | 2007

4 x 6 inches (10 x 14.5 cm)
Blown glass; hot sculpted, cut, ground
Photo by Grant Hancock

GABRIELLA DISETTO

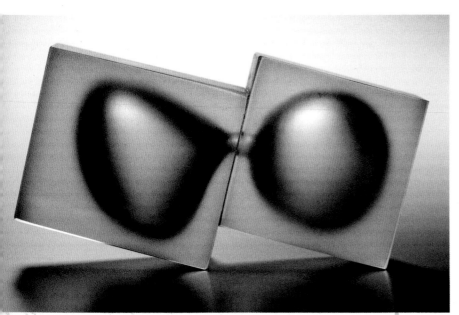

1¹⁵⁄₁₆ x 4⅛ x 1³⁄₁₆ inches
(5 x 10.5 x 3 cm)
Blown glass; cut, ground, bonded
Photo by Grant Hancock

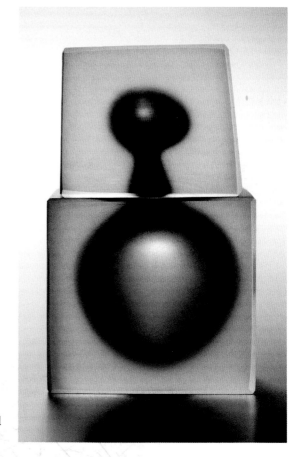

Exchange #6 | 2007 ▶

2⁹⁄₁₆ x 3¹⁵⁄₁₆ x 1³⁄₁₆ inches
(6.5 x 10 x 3 cm)
Blown glass; cut, ground, bonded
Photo by Grant Hancock

GABRIELLA PISETTO

▲ **Segment #3** │ 2006

Largest: 7½ x 10 inches (19 x 24.5 cm)
Hot glass, injected bubble; cut, ground, polished
Photo by Steve Wilson

"I grew up on a farm where it was common for us to kill livestock for the production of meat.
In this environment I learned about the internal structure of the body and became interested
in the separation that exists between the external physicality of our bodies and the concealed
organs that sustain them.**"**

▲ **The Ocean Within (60% of Body Weight Is Water)** | 2007

27⁹⁄₁₆ x 78¾ inches (70 x 200 cm)

Blown glass, hot glass

Photo by Grant Hancock

"Much of my work aims to transfer scientific and mathematical information about our bodies—the amount of air we breath, how our cells transport fluids—into visible, tangible objects by interpreting that information into glass."

▲ **Prayer to Myself (75 ml Blood/kg Body Weight)** | *2007*
Loop: 137¹³⁄₁₆ inches (350 cm)
Blown glass, paint, wire; sandblasted
Photos by Grant Hancock

Kait Rhoads

INSPIRED BY A CHILDHOOD SPENT IN THE BAHAMAS and the Caribbean, Kait Rhoads makes dreamy, fluid sculptures and vessels that bring the ocean to mind. The range of her work is diverse, and much of it possesses a hallucinatory quality and a special depth—a sense of dimension that Rhoads achieves through the layering of colored and clear glass. In the same way that water distorts shapes and provides a sense of movement, Rhoads' opaque pieces appear twisted and seem to cast shadows through their crystal-clear layers. She creates this underwater, out-of-focus quality through a careful selection of palette and patterns, displaying a developed sense of coloration.

In pieces constructed with hollow glass canes—*murrine*—Rhoads captures the multifacetedness of nature, from clouds at sunset to magnified plant parts. She cuts her blown canes and then wires them to a steel armature for support. Her approach creates a striking, otherworldly atmosphere that's akin to examining cells under a microscope. Rhoads, who has been an instructor at Pilchuck Glass School in Stanwood, Washington, and Penland School of Crafts in Penland, North Carolina, has work in collections throughout the United States.

Cherry Blossom | 2006 ▶

11 x 20¾ x 2¾ inches
(27.9 x 52.7 x 7 cm)
Blown glass, steel, powder;
murrine, cane, cut, slumped,
water-jet cut, cold worked
Photo by Robert Vinnedge

Cloud Break Small | 2008 ▶

8 x 9 x 9 inches (20.3 x 22.9 x 22.9 cm)
Blown glass; color overlay, hot de verre,
cane application

Photo by Robert Vinnedge

"Japanese kimonos are one of my main inspirations. They have a multileveled quality that's achieved through texturing, dying, painting upon, and embroidering cloth. I try to translate this quality into glass."

▼ **Chrysanthemum** | 2008

9 x 5½ x 5½ inches (22.9 x 14 x 14 cm)
Blown glass; cane application, cane drawing
Photo by Robert Vinnedge

▲ **Comb Brick** | 2008

10 x 7½ x 7½ inches (25.4 x 19.1 x 19.1 cm)
Blown glass; murrine, incalmo,
hot de verre, cane drawing
Photo by Robert Vinnedge

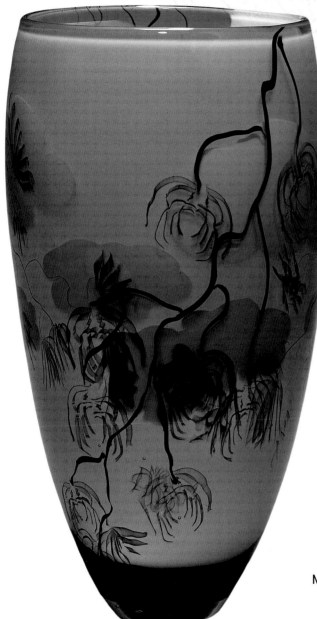

◀ **Figue** | 2008

18 x 8½ x 8½ inches (45.7 x 21.6 x 21.6 cm)
Blown glass, tank color; murrine, hot de verre,
cane drawing

Photo by Robert Vinnedge

Methuselah | 2007 ▶

16 x 9 x 7 inches
(40.6 x 22.9 x 17.8 cm)
Blown glass; zanfirico cane,
murrine

Photo by Robert Vinnedge

◄ **Aquatic Peacock** │ 2006

13 x 13 x 7 inches (33 x 33 x 17.8 cm)
Blown glass; zanfirico cane, murrine, incalmo
Photo by Robert Vinnedge

*"*I focus on the use of
foreground, middle ground,
and background in my
pieces. The thickness of the
glass allows me to create
the illusion of distance in
each work.*"*

Lunar Lagoon │ 2008 ►

9 x 10½ x 6 inches (22.9 x 26.7 x 15.2 cm)
Blown glass; zanfirico cane, murrine
Photo by Robert Vinnedge

RHOADS

KAIT

▲ **Houndstooth** │ 2007

14 x 11½ x 9½ inches (35.6 x 29.2 x 24.1 cm)

Blown glass; zanfirico cane, murrine

Photo by Robert Vinnedge

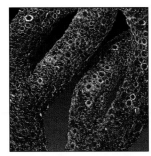

▼ **Red Polyp** | 2007

45 x 46 x 19 inches (114.3 x 116.8 x 48.3 cm)
Blown glass, copper, steel;
cut, fire polished, woven

Photos by Robert Vinnedge

▲ Rainbow Noir | 2007

    16 x 16 x 16 inches
    (40.6 x 40.6 x 40.6 cm)
    Blown glass, copper;
    cut, fire polished, woven
    Photo by Robert Vinnedge

"I love experimenting and combining different techniques to see what results. So much beauty can come from happenstance and making 'mistakes.'"

▼ Calyx | 2007

    14 x 26 x 12½ inches (35.6 x 66 x 31.8 cm)
    Blown glass, copper, steel; cut, fire polished, woven
    Photo by Robert Vinnedge

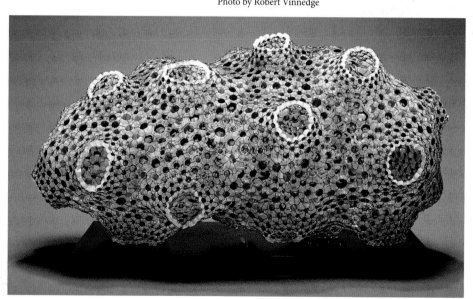

Hiroshi Yamano

YAMANO

IN COLORFUL, TRANSPARENT GLASS VESSELS that feature the ancient Asian fish motif, Japan-based artist Hiroshi Yamano distills the energy and vibrancy of nature. An iconic figure in Japanese art, the fish symbolizes movement, progress, and endurance—characteristics Yamano honors with his fluid sculptures. Dense yet luminous, weighty yet fragile, his pieces possess the loveliness associated with ornamental, decorative objects, yet they demand much more than a cursory look.

Yamano pays close attention to the angles of a fish's body and the creature's dynamic presence in its surroundings. By doing so, he instills a range of emotions—from restlessness to determination—in each sculpture. Yamano's larger pieces reference the process of hanging and drying the catch of the day—a tradition practiced in fishing cultures around the world. Updating Asian traditions in a way that's fresh and intimate, Yamano's work is an unforgettable combination of ancient and modern creative modes. He lives in Awara, Japan.

From East to West, Fish Catcher #583 | 2008 ▶

4⁵⁄₁₆ x 8¼ x 8¹⁄₁₆ inches (11 x 21 x 20.5 cm)
Blown glass, copper plating; cut, engraved

Photo by artist

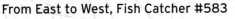

▲ **From East to West, Nagare #55** | 2008

11⅝ x 11⅜ x 10⁷⁄₁₆ inches (29.5 x 29 x 26.5 cm)

Blown glass, copper plating; cut, engraved

Photo by artist

▲ **From East to West, Fish Hanger #102** | 2005

22¹⁄₁₆ x 22⁷⁄₁₆ x ⅞ inches (56 x 57 x 15 cm)
Blown glass, copper plating, steel; cut, engraved
Photo by artist

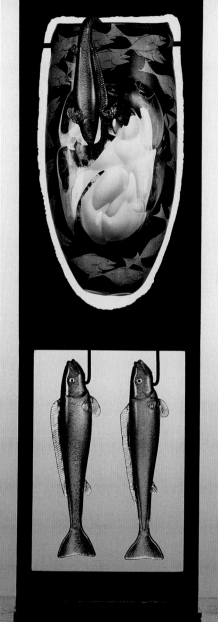

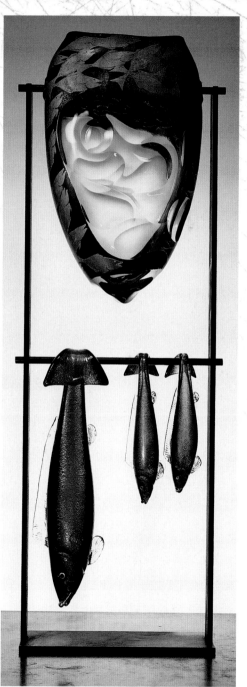

From East to West, Fish Hanger #21 | 2003 ►

39⅜ x 12⅝ x 4¹⁵⁄₁₆ inches
(100 x 32.1 x 12.5 cm)
Blown glass, copper plating,
steel; cut, engraved

Photo by artist

"I look carefully at
my blown pieces
and let each of them
guide me through the
creative process. An
individual work will
send me in a direction
that's unique."

▲ From East to West, Fish Hanger #100 | 2005

33⁷⁄₁₆ x 11¹³⁄₁₆ x 5⅞ inches (85 x 30 x 15 cm)
Blown glass, copper plating, steel; cut, engraved

Photo by artist

HIROSHI YAMANO

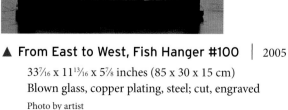

▲ **From East to West, Nagare #110** | 2009

15¹⁵⁄₁₆ x 8⅞ x 3⁵⁄₁₆ inches (40.5 x 22.5 x 8.5 cm)

Blown glass, copper plating; cut, engraved

Photo by artist

▲ **From East to West, Nagare #61** | 2008

18 ¹¹⁄₁₆ x 10¼ x 7¹¹⁄₁₆ inches (47.5 x 26 x 19.5 cm)

Blown glass, copper plating; cut, engraved

Photo by artist

"I'm inspired by fish like tuna or mackerel that swim in order to stay alive. If they stop, they die. I think of myself as a fish—I have to keep working, keep going, keep jumping into life."

◀ **From East to West, Fish Hanger #119** │ 2006

20⅞ x 12⁹⁄₁₆ x 9¹³⁄₁₆ inches (53 x 32 x 25 cm)
Blown glass, copper plating, stone, steel;
cut, engraved

Photo by artist

HIROSHI YAMANO

"I'm an artist who loves

to dance with molten glass.**"**

▲ **From East to West, Nagare #88** │ 2008

14⁹⁄₁₆ x 13¾ x 13⅜ inches (37 x 35 x 34 cm)
Blown glass, copper plating; cut, engraved
Photo by artist

▲ **From East to West, Nagare #108** │ 2009

9⅝ x 14³⁄₁₆ x 13 inches (24.5 x 36 x 33 cm)
Blown glass, copper plating; cut, engraved
Photo by artist

▲ From East to West, Nagare #89 | 2008

14⅜ x 13¾ x 11 inches (36.5 x 35 x 28 cm)
Blown glass, copper plating; cut, engraved
Photo by artist

◀ From East to West, Nagare #84 | 2008

10 x 9⅝ x 6⅞ inches (25.5 x 24.5 x 17.5 cm)
Blown glass, copper plating; cut, engraved
Photo by artist

William Gudenrath

FROM WINE GOBLETS WITH SPIRALING STEMS and precise air twists to octagonal drinking glasses wrapped simply at their lips with bands of color, the distinctive glassware of William Gudenrath has an understated elegance. His pieces are thin walled and delicate yet braced by smart proportions and balanced curves. Unlike many glassblowers, Gudenrath works without a team. The solitude has made it possible for him to proceed at his own pace with form and color and to research the history of glassblowing. His experiments with the vessel have resulted in timeless pieces that reflect his deep understanding of culturally significant forms.

The expertise and control Gudenrath brings to his craft have allowed him to develop a signature style, with recognizable flourishes such as the dragon motif and the densely coiled knots that frequently appear in his work. An authority on hot glassworking techniques from ancient Egypt through the Renaissance, Gudenrath gives lectures and demonstrations around the world. He lives in New York.

▼ **Ming-Style Bowls** | 2007

Each: 7 inches (17.8 cm) in diameter
Blown glass
Photo by Harry Seaman

▲ **Historical Riot** | 2008

Tallest: 13 inches (33 cm)
Blown glass

Photo by Ann Cady

▲ Octagonal Tumblers, Bowls, and Vase | 1997

Tallest: 7 inches (17.8 cm)
Blown glass

Photo by Harry Seaman

"I'm so torn: Is my real favorite 'look' minimalist or baroque? Fortunately, I don't have to pick one over the other. Some modernist galleries would be shocked to see my other side. I hope they never Google me."

◀ **Air-Twist Stemmed Champagne Flutes** | 2003

Each: 10 inches (25.4 cm) tall
Blown glass
Photo by Ann Cady

◀ **Two Lead Crystal Goblets for Steuben** | 1997

Tallest: 10 inches (25.4 cm)
Lead crystal, gold leaf
Photo by Ann Cady

▼ **Candlesticks and Compote** | 2006

Tallest candlestick: 7 inches (17.8 cm)
Bowl: 7 inches (17.8 cm) in diameter
Blown glass, gold leaf
Photo by Harry Seaman

"Blowing glass at the furnace is one of the most interesting and unusual of human activities, just from a movement point of view. It really is a sort of non-rhythmic dance."

▼ Lidded Dragon Goblet | 1998
24 inches (61 cm) tall
Blown glass
Photo by Harry Seaman

▼ Fiery Dragon Goblet | 2007
12 inches (30.5 cm) tall
Blown glass
Photo by Michael Schwartz

▲ **Lidded Dragons** | 2003
Each: 13 inches (33 cm) tall
Blown glass
Photo by Harry Seaman

◀ **Lidded Dragon Goblet and Carafe** | 2002
Tallest: 21 inches (53.3 cm)
Blown glass, gold leaf
Photo by Nick Williams

"When I was eleven, I first softened glass tubing over a flame. Forty-eight years later, I'm still amazed—almost disbelieving—when glass makes that magical transformation.**"**

▼ **Sea-Green Centerpieces** | 2003
Tallest: 13 inches (33 cm)
Blown glass
Photo by Harry Seaman

▼ **Sea-Green Trio** | 2008
Tallest: 11 inches (27.9 cm)
Blown glass
Photo by Harry Seaman

MARQUIS

Richard Marquis

ONE OF THE FIRST AMERICAN GLASS ARTISTS to visit the island of Murano in the 1960s, Richard Marquis observed firsthand the intricate Venetian techniques executed there by master glassblowers. The *encalmo*, *filigrana*, *murrine*, and *zanfirico* procedures he learned from those Italian experts he readily and generously shared with others, and they continue to be central to his own work. Over the years, Marquis' contributions to the contemporary studio-glass movement as a creator and a teacher have been vast.

Few artists use glass as engagingly as Marquis does. A master of moods, he has produced a body of work that runs the gamut from zany, madcap sculptural objects to carefully conceived teapots that are an homage to Venetian glass masters. Whatever their intention, his pieces always exhibit discipline, integrity, and wit. Marquis, who lives in Washington state, has received numerous grants and honors, among them the Smithsonian Institute's James Renwick Alliance Masters of the Medium Award. His work is held in institutions worldwide, including the Metropolitan Museum of Art in New York City and the Victoria and Albert Museum in London.

Large Egg on Wheels, 09-3 | 2009 ▶
9½ x 14½ x 10½ inches
(24.1 x 36.8 x 26.7 cm)
Glass, brass, steel, rubber, paint;
granulare technique
Photo by artist

▲ **Eggs in Cages** | 2009

Largest: 17½ x 12 x 12 inches (44.5 x 30.5 x 30.5 cm)
Glass, found objects; granulare technique

Photo by artist

▲ **Stars and Stripes Teapots** | 1997

Tallest: 8 inches (20.3 cm)
Glass; murrine, a canne technique, encalmo
Photo by artist

◀ **Granulare Birds and Eggs** | 2005

Tallest: 15 inches (38.1 cm)
Glass; granulare technique
Photo by artist

"I think that out of all the basic geometric shapes, the cone delivers the most artistic punch."

◀ **Witch's Hat** | 2008
12 x 12 x 12 inches (30.5 x 30.5 x 30.5 cm)
Glass; hot-slab constructed, wheel carved
Photo by artist

▲ **Razzle-Dazzle Boat** | 2008
5½ x 19¼ x 5¾ inches (13.9 x 48.9 x 14.6 cm)
Glass; hot-slab constructed, wheel carved
Photo by artist

▼ **Whole Elk Garage, 08-3** | 2008

6¼ x 11 x 11 inches (15.9 x 27.9 x 27.9 cm)
Glass, found object; hot-slab constructed,
whole-elk technique, wheel carved

Photo by artist

"The Whole Elk Theory states that if you kill an elk you must use everything—
hooves, tail, teeth. My piece *Whole Elk Garage* uses leftover by-products
from some of my other work.**"**

RICHARD MARQUIS

Dick's Works | 2007 ▶

Each: 10½ x 16 x 6½ inches
(26.7 x 40.6 x 16.5 cm)
Glass, found objects;
granulare technique

Photo by artist

◀ **Sphere Pyramid** | 2006

18 x 18 x 18 inches
(45.7 x 45.7 x 45.7 cm)
Glass, wood; granulare technique

Photo by artist

RICHARD MARQUIS

▼ **Land Speed Assault Vehicle, 07-3** | 2007

6 x 26 x 10 inches (15.2 x 66 x 25.4 cm)
Glass, brass, wood, gesso; a canne technique
Photo by artist

◄ **Marquiscarpa** | 2004

5¾ x 7½ x 3 inches
(14.6 x 19 x 7.6 cm)
Blown glass; fused, slumped,
wheel carved, murrine
Photo by artist

"A fascination with things that go fast inspired my land speed assault vehicles. I attend the Bonneville Salt Flat runs in Utah when I can."

▲ **Land Speed Assault Vehicles (LSAVs)** | 2007

Each: 6 x 26 x 10 inches (15.2 x 66 x 25.4 cm)
Glass, brass, wood, gesso; a canne technique
Photo by artist

Nick Mount

LOOKING AT A SCENT BOTTLE MADE BY Australian glassblower Nick Mount is like looking at a dancer: Both have long lines and colorful exteriors. Both are animated and dramatic. Each of Mount's bottles has a distinct personality, and when assembled into a group, the pieces manifest a variety of relationships. Their playful forms seem to take on human traits—whimsy, sobriety, dignity, flirtatiousness—and they feature a delightful range of colors: soft pinks and muted blues, vibrant tangerines and dazzling reds.

Mount sets up complementary relationships between the wispy projections and sleek lines that comprise his designs, establishing perfectly balanced proportions. He has redefined traditional Venetian glass techniques to create his own distinctive style. Using a tasteful mix of *filigrana*, *murrine*, and colored glass elements, he creates works that have a unique aesthetic—a combination of elegant refinement and idiosyncratic wit. With nearly four decades of glassblowing experience, Mount is well known throughout Europe, Japan, and the United States for his commissions, teaching, and exhibitions.

▲ **Scent Bottle: Tacoma Dome** | 2007
28 x 70 x 12 inches (71.1 x 177.8 x 30.5 cm)
Blown glass, found objects, enamel; surface worked, sgraffito
Photo by Richard Marquis

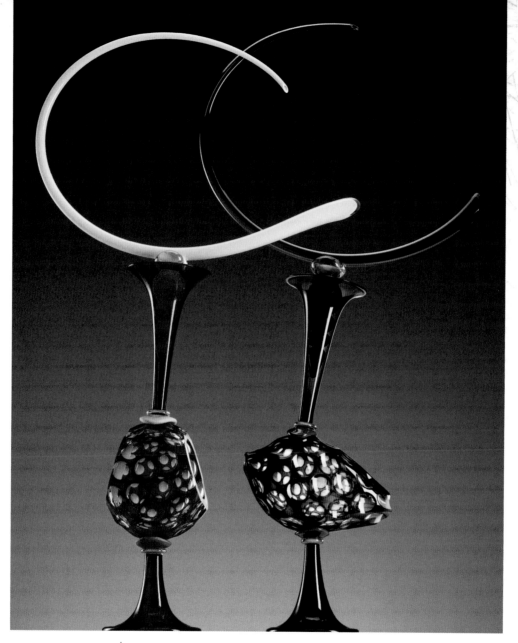

▲ **Scent Bottles** | 2008

    Tallest: 42 x 22 x 6 inches (106.7 x 55.9 x 15.2 cm)

    Blown glass; carved, polished, assembled

    Photo by Grant Hancock

▲ **Scent Bottle: Tacoma Dome** | 2007

27 x 44 x 10 inches (68.6 x 111.8 x 25.4 cm)
Blown glass, enamel, found objects;
sgraffito, surface worked

Photo by Richard Marquis

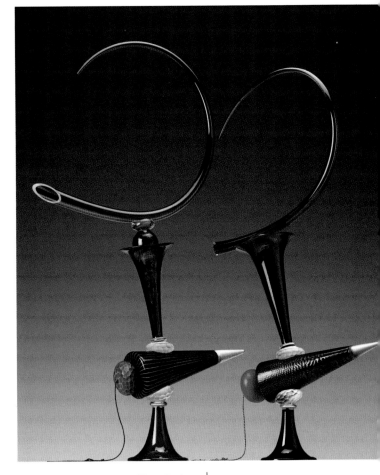

▲ **Scent Bottles: Falling Bobs** | 2008

Largest: 22 x 40 x 5½ inches (55.9 x 101.6 x 14 cm)
Blown glass, silk thread; carved, polished, assembled

Photo by Grant Hancock

"Tools are important to me as indicators of a process, as a symbol of the link that exists between the hand and the medium."

◀ **Scent Bottle** | 2008
42½ x 23 x 6 inches (108 x 58.4 x 15.2 cm)
Blown glass; carved, polished, assembled
Photo by Grant Hancock

NICK MOUNT

"Assembling the scent bottle components is a symbiosis of the experimental and the historical. I counterbalance transparency with opacity, delicacy with vibrancy, and the attenuated with the voluptuous."

▲ **Scent Bottles** | 2003

Tallest: 34½ x 7 x 7 inches (87.6 x 17.8 x 17.8 cm)
Blown glass, enamel, pencil, mild steel spike;
murrine, carved, assembled
Photo by Grant Hancock

▲ **Scent Bottles** | 2005

Tallest: 15½ x 10 x 4½ inches
(39.4 x 25.4 x 11.4 cm)
Blown glass; carved, polished, assembled
Photo by Grant Hancock

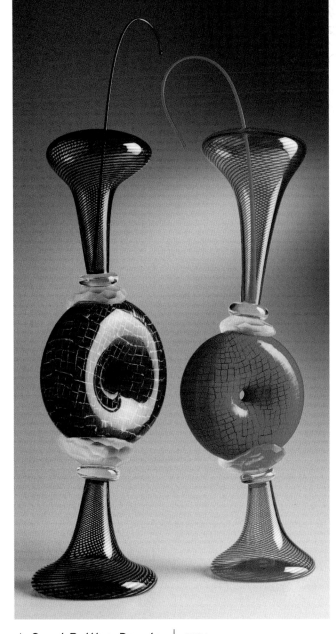

▲ Scent Bottles: Donuts | 2004

Largest: 19 x 4½ x 4 inches (48.3 x 11.4 x 10.2 cm)
Blown glass; murrine, carved, polished, assembled

Photo by Grant Hancock

▲ Scent Bottles: Donuts | 2004

Tallest: 17 x 6 x 5½ inches (43.2 x 15.2 x 14 cm)
Blown glass; murrine, assembled

Photo by Grant Hancock

NICK MOUNT

"My forms are derived from both a fundamental engagement with process and the intrinsic qualities of the medium."

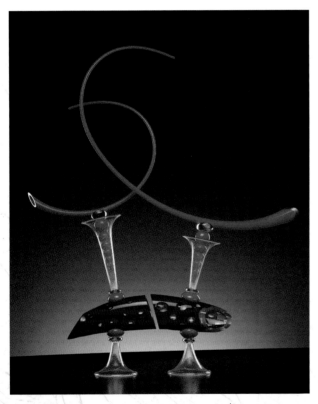

▲ Scent Bottle: Combination Piece | 2007
42 x 36½ x 7½ inches (106.7 x 92.7 x 19.1 cm)
Blown glass; carved, polished, assembled
Photo by Grant Hancock

▲ Scent Bottle: Combination Piece | 2008
37 x 31 x 6¾ inches (94 x 78.7 x 17.1 cm)
Blown glass; carved, polished, assembled
Photo by Grant Hancock

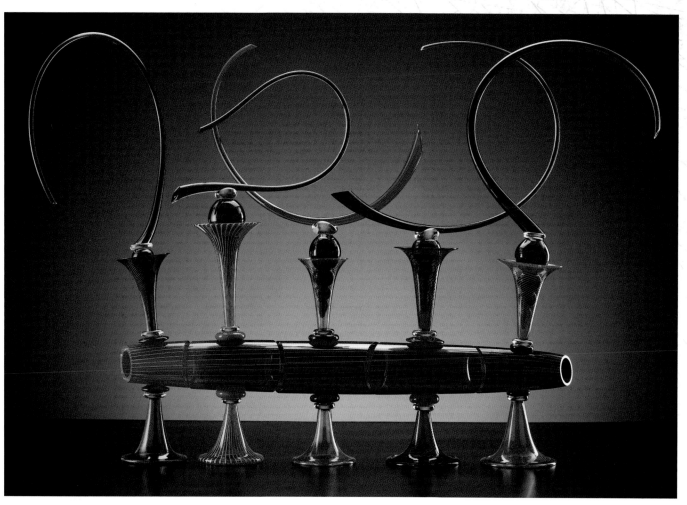

▲ Scent Bottle: Combination Piece | 2007

32 x 56 x 16 inches (81.3 x 142.2 x 40.6 cm)
Blown glass; polished, assembled

Photo by Grant Hancock

Peter Houk

THE DYNAMICS OF CROWDED SPACES as they're altered by construction and destruction provide Peter Houk with images for his luminous vessels. Some of Houk's pieces refer specifically to an attempt by the city of Boston, Massachusetts, to force traffic underground, but the works bring to mind more general urban renewal projects that are occurring worldwide. Houk makes the grit and grandeur of such undertakings palpable in the haunting, silhouetted skylines that envelope the pieces. He renders these images with a printmaker's sensibility. To transfer the images onto glass for sandblasting, Houk uses a cold-working technique called graal. He inks the carved surface of a piece with enamel paint, then covers it with an encasement of clear glass, which he blows to the desired shape and size.

Houk's other works often feature words, letters, and natural motifs—leaves and twigs that he collects from forests and beaches. Houk is inspired by the complex patterns present in both natural and urban systems, and he brings out the innate beauty of both in his engaging work. His pieces are in many private and public collections, including the Corning Museum of Glass in Corning, New York, and the Museum of American Glass in Millville, New Jersey. He lives in Medford, Massachusetts.

Big Dig #66 | 2008 ▶
11 x 10 inches (27.9 x 25.4 cm)
Blown glass, vitreous paint; incalmo, sandblasted, painted
Photo by James Beards

◀ **Big Dig #61** | 2009

18 x 10 inches (45.7 x 25.4 cm)
Blown glass, vitreous paint;
sandblasted, painted

Photo by Bill Truslow

▲ **Big Dig #13** | 1997

12 x 9 inches (30.5 x 22.9 cm)
Blown glass, vitreous paint;
sandblasted, painted

Photo by James Beards

"I'm always working toward the point
where image and glass are equal partners
and therefore inseparable."

▼ **Big Dig #39** | 2005

14 x 8 inches (35.6 x 20.3 cm)
Blown glass, vitreous paint;
sandblasted, painted

Photo by Bill Truslow

Ceci N'est Pas Un Vaisseau | 2008 ▶

10 x 21 x 5 inches (25.4 x 53.3 x 12.7 cm)
Blown glass, wood; sandblasted

Photo by James Beards

▼ Entropia | 2008

Tallest: 15 inches (38.1 cm)
Blown glass, enamel; sandblasted

Photo by Bill Truslow

▲ **Leaves and Protozoans** | 1998

16 x 9 inches (40.6 x 22.9 cm)
Blown glass, vitreous paint;
sandblasted, painted

Photo by James Beards

▲ **Frost** | 1996

14 x 5½ inches (35.6 x 14 cm)
Blown glass, vitreous paint;
sandblasted, painted

Photo by James Beards

Sandblasted Platters | 1997 ▶

Each: 23 inches
(12.7 cm) in diameter
Blown glass; sandblasted

Photos by James Beards

"Glass is too pure and sacred for me to feel comfortable with . . . unless I can mess it up a little."

◀ **Leaf Bowl** | 2009

10 inches (25.4 cm) in diameter
Blown glass; sandblasted

Photos by Bill Truslow

PETER HOUK

"The play between glass and changing light gives rise to a range of ephemeral phenomena, including reflection, refraction, and projection. I'm interested in exploring these phenomena, especially the ones that lie at the edge of our ability to perceive them."

Big Dig #18 | 1999 ▶

13 x 8½ inches (33 x 21.6 cm)
Blown glass, vitreous paint;
sandblasted, painted

Photo by James Beards

◀ **Big Dig #58** | 2009

12 x 9 inches (30.5 x 22.9 cm)
Blown glass, vitreous paint;
sandblasted, painted

Photo by Bill Truslow

PETER HOUK

Jane Bruce

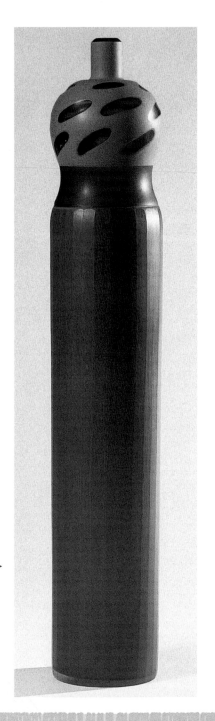

AGGRESSIVELY EXPLORING THE TRADITIONAL DEFINITIONS
of art and craft, Jane Bruce challenges the standard meanings of these two
categories and examines the controversial middle ground that exists between
them. Her recent work features bottle forms blown by art students in Australia.
Bruce cold-works the bottles, cutting and engraving decorative elements
onto their surfaces to systematically expose the layer of color beneath. The
refinement of her decoration and the rhythm of its placement around each
bottle subtly enhance the optical properties of the glass.

Bruce produces objects that are both pleasing to the eye and exude the well-
mastered poise of royal guards; their stateliness captures the quiet confidence
of a sentry standing on watch. Bruce, who lives in New York City, has received
a wide range of awards and fellowships. Her work can be found in prestigious
collections worldwide, including those of the Victoria and Albert Museum
in London, the Corning Museum of Glass in Corning, New York, and the
Queensland Art Gallery in Brisbane, Australia.

Yellow/Blue Sentinel | 2004 ▶
33$\frac{1}{16}$ x 5$\frac{1}{2}$ x 5$\frac{1}{2}$ inches
(84 x 14 x 14 cm)
Blown glass; wheel cut
Photo by David Patterson

◀ **Ivory/Cream Sentinel** │ 2003

$21^5/8$ x $4^{11}/_{16}$ x $4^{11}/_{16}$ inches
(55 x 12 x 12 cm)
Blown glass; wheel cut

Photo by David Patterson

"I'm interested in the 'essential' object—

in reducing a piece to its fundamental parts.**"**

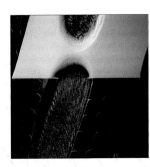

Grey/Primrose Sentinel | 2003 ▶

30¹¹⁄₁₆ x 5⅞ x 5⅞ inches (78 x 15 x 15 cm)
Blown glass; wheel cut,
engraved, sandblasted

Photos by David Patterson

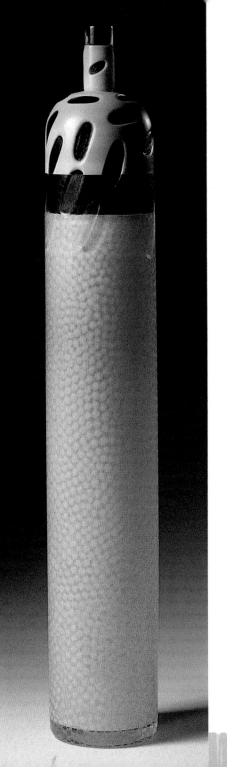

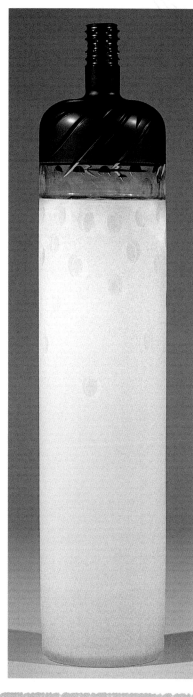

White/Black Sentinel | 2003 ▶

23⅝ x 4⁵⁄₁₆ x 4⁵⁄₁₆ inches
(60 x 11 x 11 cm)
Blown glass; wheel cut, sandblasted

Photo by David Patterson

◀ **Black/Clear/White Sentinel** | 2004

29⅛ x 5½ x 5½ inches
(74 x 14 x 14 cm)
Blown glass; wheel cut

Photo by David Patterson

JANE **BRUCE**

White/White Sentinel | 2003 ▶

31¹⁄₁₆ x 5⁵⁄₁₆ x 5⁵⁄₁₆ inches
(79 x 13.5 x 13.5 cm)
Blown glass; wheel cut
Photo by David Patterson

"With the *Sentinels* series
I wanted to investigate
and to change the viewer's
relationship to the work—
to examine the space
between the work and
the viewer.**"**

◀ **White/Primrose Sentinel** | 2003

32⁷⁄₁₆ x 4⁵⁄₁₆ x 4⁵⁄₁₆ inches
(82.5 x 11 x 11 cm)
Blown glass; wheel cut
Photo by David Patterson

◀ **Salmon/Black Sentinel** | 2003

31 x 6¼ x 6¼ inches
(78.7 x 15.9 x 15.9 cm)
Blown glass; wheel cut

Photo by David Patterson

Yellow/Yellow Sentinel | 2003 ▶

27¹⁵⁄₁₆ x 4¹⁵⁄₁₆ x 4¹⁵⁄₁₆ inches
(71 x 12.5 x 12.5 cm)
Blown glass; wheel cut

Photo by David Patterson

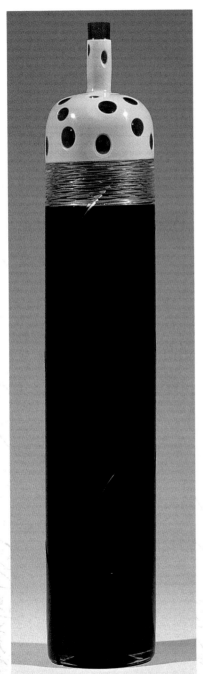

◀ **Celadon/Black Sentinel** | 2004

31⅞ x 5½ x 5½ inches
(81 x 14 x 14 cm)
Blown glass; wheel cut

Photo by David Patterson

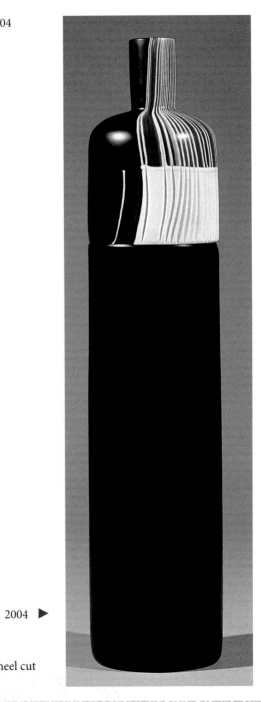

Vanilla/Black Sentinel | 2004 ▶

29¹⁵⁄₁₆ x 5¹¹⁄₁₆ x 5¹¹⁄₁₆ inches
(76 x 14.4 x 14.4 cm)
Blown glass; kiln formed, wheel cut

Photo by David Patterson

"I'm fascinated by the shifting, liminal space that exists between craft and art, function and non-function. Selecting ingredients from each world, I create hybrid objects that explore this space."

◀ **Black/White Sentinel** │ 2004

23³⁄₁₆ x 4⅛ x 4⅛ inches (59 x 10.5 x 10.5 cm)

Blown glass; wheel cut

Photos by David Patterson

Wendy Fairclough

IN HER PRECISELY ARRANGED COMPOSITIONS of modest household items—blown-glass versions of measuring cups and buckets, funnels and teapots—Wendy Fairclough creates remarkably compelling still lifes that take the viewer by surprise. The pieces themselves may bring to mind workaday chores or home maintenance, but the colors in which Fairclough renders them—appealing pastels and bright whites—dramatically alter the dynamic of each piece.

Paying tribute to the commonplace, Fairclough creates simple pieces that have a sophisticated twist. Her household tableaux—arrangements of glass rags and mops, dishes and fruit—reflect a receptive sensibility, one that's open to humor and surreal suggestion. Through her artful assemblages of familiar objects, she instills the material world as we know it with a distinctive resonance. Fairclough's work is represented in numerous private and public collections, including the National Art Glass Collection of the Wagga Wagga Art Gallery in Wagga Wagga, Australia, and the Museum of New Zealand Te Papa Tongarewa in Wellington, New Zealand. Her studio-based glass practice is located in the Adelaide Hills of South Australia.

▼ **Kumarangk** | 2008

6¹¹⁄₁₆ x 34⁵⁄₈ x 11¹³⁄₁₆ inches (17 x 88 x 30 cm)
Blown glass, enamel paint; sandblasted, engraved, hand lapped, oiled
Photo by Grant Hancock

▲ **Acquiescence** | 2009

40⅛ x 78¾ x 59⅟₁₆ inches (102 x 200 x 150 cm)

Blown glass, acrylic bucket handles, found stepladder and broom, acrylic paint; sandblasted

Photo by Grant Hancock

▲ **Shelf Life** | 2008

13³⁄₁₆ x 29¹⁵⁄₁₆ x 14⁹⁄₁₆ inches (33.5 x 76 x 37 cm)

Blown glass; carved, laminated, sandblasted, oiled

Photo by Grant Hancock

▲ **Joy** | 2007

11³⁄₈ x 37³⁄₈ x 13¾ inches (29 x 95 x 35 cm)

Blown glass; sandblasted

Photo by Grant Hancock

"I enjoy arranging objects so that they create a narrative—in essence, a fiction."

▲ **Shades of Green** | 2008

15⅛ x 41⁵⁄₁₆ x 18⅛ inches (38.5 x 105 x 46 cm)

Blown glass; sandblasted, hand lapped

Photo by Grant Hancock

"Referencing domestic objects in my work allows viewers to immediately identify with it and bring their own stories and understandings to it."

▲ **Grey Days** | 2008

15⁵⁄₁₆ x 35⁷⁄₁₆ x 21¼ inches (39 x 90 x 54 cm)
Blown glass; sandblasted, hand lapped
Photo by Grant Hancock

▲ **Point of Arrival, After William Fox** | 2007

12³⁄₁₆ x 46⁷⁄₁₆ x 9¹³⁄₁₆ inches (31 x 118 x 25 cm)
Blown glass, enamel paint; sandblasted, engraved, hand lapped
Photo by Grant Hancock

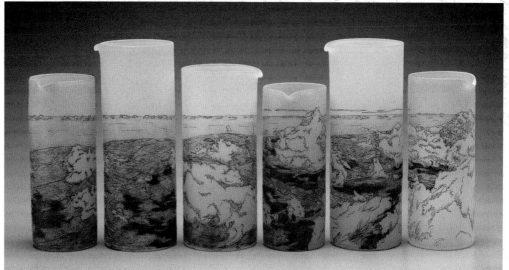

Leaving | 2006 ▶

13¾ x 30¹¹⁄₁₆ x 5⅞ inches
(35 x 78 x 15 cm)
Blown glass, enamel paint;
sandblasted, engraved,
hand lapped

Photos by Grant Hancock

▲ **Journey** | 2006

18⅛ x 39⅜ x 11 inches (46 x 100 x 28 cm)
Blown glass, enamel paint; sandblasted, engraved, hand lapped

Photos by Grant Hancock

▼ **Still Life with Table** │ 2006

38⁹⁄₁₆ x 53⅛ x 43⁵⁄₁₆ inches (98 x 135 x 110 cm)
Blown glass, wooden table, metal milk holder, acrylic paint; sandblasted
Photos by Grant Hancock

"I don't like the glossy surface of glass. I find it hard to read a form when light is bouncing off of it. Sandblasting pares a form down and mutes it, altering it in a way that retains translucency. It gives my pieces a dreamlike quality.**"**

◀ **Next to Godliness** | 2006

51³⁄₁₆ x 59¹⁄₁₆ x 13¾ inches
(130 x 150 x 35 cm)
Blown glass, cast glass,
acrylic handles, wooden bench;
sandblasted

Photos by Grant Hancock

Sonja Blomdahl

IN VESSELS AND SCULPTURAL OBJECTS THAT epitomize harmony and proportion, Washington state artist Sonja Blomdahl exhibits her mastery of the *incalmo* technique. Using this classic Italian method, Blomdahl constructs her vessels by fusing bands comprised of two or more blown-glass pieces. The edges of each glass element must be identical in diameter before the pieces can be joined, which requires a high level of skill and precision on the part of the artist. In addition to their seamless joints, Blomdahl's vessels feature wondrous color combinations and supple curves.

Through her use of opaque and transparent glasses, Blomdahl plays with light in her work, highlighting the lovely proportions for which she's known. To add surface texture to her pieces, she employs cold-work etching, using this process to create lines that contrast beautifully with the smooth glassiness of the rest of the work. Indulgent in color, shape, and form, her vessels are nothing short of lavish. Blomdahl, who is married to artist Dick Weiss, has work in permanent collections worldwide, including the Boston Museum of Fine Arts in Boston, the Clinton Presidential Library and Museum in Little Rock, Arkansas, and the Museum of Decorative Art in Prague, Czech Republic.

◀ **Cobalt/Red-Yellow** │ 1983
7 x 14 inches (17.8 x 35.6 cm)
Blown glass; incalmo
Photo by Lynn Thompson

▲ **Gold/Iris, Aqua/Red-Yellow, Autumn/Leaf, Honey/Red** | 2006

Largest: 11 x 13½ inches (27.9 x 34.3 cm)

Blown glass; incalmo, battuto

Photo by Russell Johnson

"As an artist, my focus is the vessel. If I have done my work correctly, a vessel's profile will be a continuous curve, its shape will be full, and its opening will be confident."

▲ **Golden Blue/Amber/Lime** | 2001

19 x 13 inches (48.3 x 33 cm)
Blown glass; incalmo, battuto
Photo by Lynn Thompson

◄ **Red/Yellow/Turquoise** | 1999

12½ x 12 inches (31.8 x 30.5 cm)
Blown glass; incalmo
Photo by Lynn Thompson

Apricot/Aubergine | 2003 ▶

7½ x 13½ inches (19.1 x 34.3 cm)
Blown glass; incalmo
Photo by Lynn Thompson

◀ **Mandarin/Violet** | 2002

9¼ x 11 inches (23.5 x 27.9 cm)
Blown glass; incalmo, battuto
Photo by Lynn Thompson

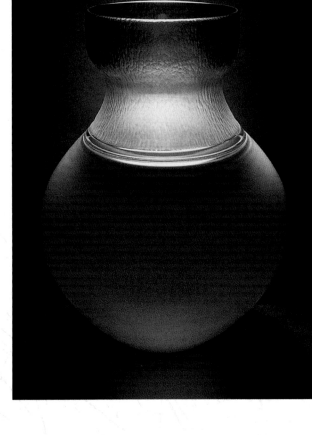

◀ **Marble/Ice Blue** │ 2001

15 x 11 inches (38.1 x 27.9 cm)
Blown glass; incalmo, battuto
Photo by Lynn Thompson

Coral/Pearl Blue, Opal/Pink Pearl │ 2000 ▶

Left: 16¼ x 11 inches (41.3 x 27.9 cm)
Right: 17½ x 11 inches (44.5 x 27.9 cm)
Blown glass; incalmo
Photo by Lynn Thompson

"Glassblowing is a process charged with immediacy. The procedure requires rapid decisions at many different points, and toward the end each motion becomes crucial. To challenge myself, I like to be at a point that's just beyond my control."

▲ Citrus/Amber | 2002

6¼ x 12 inches (15.9 x 30.5 cm)
Blown glass; incalmo, battuto

Photo by Lynn Thompson

▲ Mandarin/Amethyst | 2005
10½ x 10½ inches (26.6 x 26.6 cm)
Blown glass; incalmo, battuto
Photo by Lynn Thompson

"In a sense, any piece that I create is a history of my breath."

▲ Copper Blue/Aqua | 1998
14¾ x 12 inches (37.5 x 30.5 cm)
Blown glass; incalmo
Photo by Lynn Thompson

◀ **Aqua/Scarlet** | 2005

14½ x 11¼ inches
(36.8 x 28.6 cm)
Blown glass; incalmo, battuto
Photo by Lynn Thompson

Michael Rogers

ESTABLISHING REVELATORY JUXTAPOSITIONS using glass, found objects, and text, Michael Rogers creates symbolic, highly literary pieces that engage the viewer on a number of levels. Much of Rogers' work is inspired by his wide and varied reading and his appreciation for the poetics of language. He often engraves text onto his glass pieces, wrapping passages of words around his vessels, whirlwind fashion, like a cascade of thought.

Rogers rarely uses color in his sculptures, preferring to play up the transparent quality of glass. His provocative incorporation of found objects and antiques grounds each work, creating a bond between it and material culture. Inspired constellations of thoughts and ideas, Rogers' precisely assembled sculptures are rich, poignant, and complex. His work can be found in the permanent collections of the Suntory Museum of Art in Tokyo, Japan, the First Contemporary Glass Museum in Madrid, Spain, and the Museo del Vidrio in Monterrey, Mexico. He lives and works in upstate New York.

Beehive for Molly Bloom | 2001 ▶

20 x 10 x 10 inches
(50.8 x 25.4 x 25.4 cm)
Glass, beeswax
Photo by Bette Rogers

▲ **Flight Remembered** | 2008

21 x 20 x 20 inches (53.3 x 50.8 x 50.8 cm)

Glass, cast glass elements, water

Photos by Geoff Tesch

▲ **Sisters** | 2007

20 x 8 x 8 inches (50.8 x 20.3 x 20.3 cm)

Glass, found object

Photos by Geoff Tesch

▲ **Invisible Cities** | 2000

15 x 8 x 8 inches (38.1 x 20.3 x 20.3 cm)

Glass, cast elements

Photo by Bette Rogers

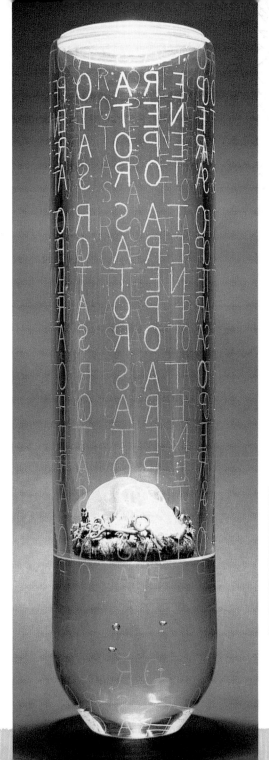

"I'm very interested in the layering of visual information. Like ancient palimpsests, where writing can be read behind layer after layer of writing, glass is the perfect medium for expressing overlays of information."

◄ **Cipher** | 2001
22 x 6 x 6 inches (55.9 x 15.2 x 15.2 cm)
Glass, cast elements, steel powder, keys, magnet
Photos by Bette Rogers

MICHAEL **ROGERS**

147

"I appreciate the lyrical quality of glassblowing. There aren't many processes that require the breath of the maker to create a form."

The Writer's Instruments | 2009 ▶

75 x 85 x 8 inches
(190.5 x 215.9 x 20.3 cm)
Glass, water

Photos by Geoff Tesch

ROGERS

MICHAEL

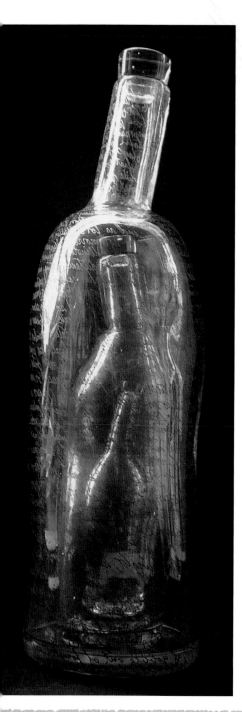

◀ **Finnegan's Wake Bar Scene** | 2000

19 x 6 x 6 inches
(48.3 x 15.2 x 15.2 cm)
Glass

Photos by Bette Rogers

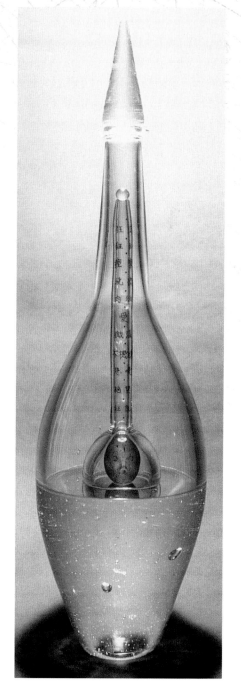

Scale of Emotions | 2000 ▶

20 x 7 x 7 inches
(50.8 x 17.8 x 17.8 cm)
Glass, cast elements; engraved

Photo by Bette Rogers

MICHAEL ROGERS

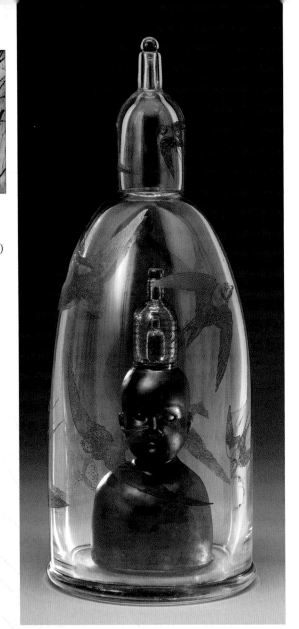

In Flight | 2007 ▶

23½ x 9½ x 9½ inches
(59.7 x 24.1 x 24.1 cm)
Glass, cast elements

Photos by Geoff Tesch

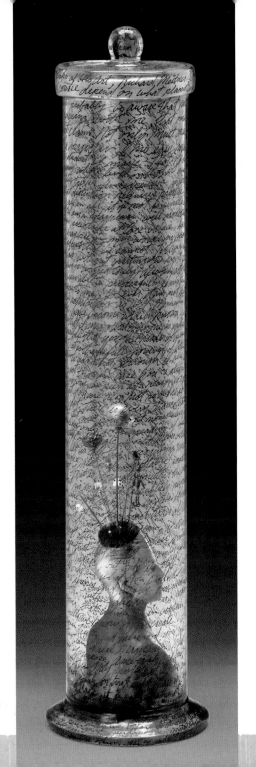

Portrait of Meitner | 2006 ▶

16 x 5 x 5 inches
(40.6 x 12.7 x 12.7 cm)Glass, found objects
Photo by Geoff Tesch

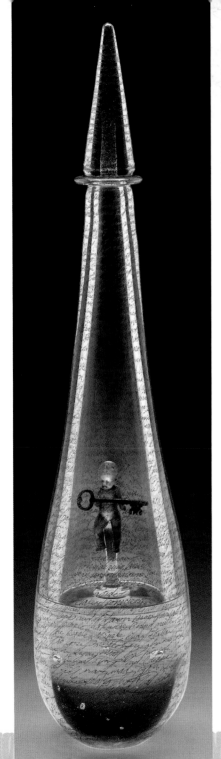

◀ **Yeats' Key** | 2007

28 x 6 x 6 inches
(71.1 x 15.2 x 15.2 cm)
Glass, brass lion, magnet,
iron powder

Photos by Geoff Tesch

▲ **Telling the Bees** | 2008

21 x 15 x 15 inches
(53.3 x 38.1 x 38.1 cm)
Glass, cast elements, thread, key

Photo by Geoff Tesch

"Making art is my way of trying to hold on to the ephemera of daily life. Glass, with its transparency and translucency as a material, is at once there and not there, making it the perfect poetic material for trying to capture the fleeting."

MOORE

Benjamin P. Moore

FEATURING FORMS AND COLORS THAT ARE REMARKABLY PURE, the work of Benjamin Moore has a sophistication that's at once old fashioned and of the moment. Designed with carefully calculated simplicity, his bowls and vases feature fluid, elegantly integrated contours. He brings these same characteristics to his collaborative work on chandeliers and wall pieces. Although they're more decorative in design, these pieces play with the concept of geometric shape and engage the functional aspects of glass' translucency.

Through the allure of carefully executed lines and a sense of serenity and unity, Moore's refined, harmonious works entice the viewer. As an artist and an instructor, he has contributed profoundly to the studio glass movement, creating opportunities for Italian masters from Murano to teach Venetian glassblowing techniques in the United States. His work is featured in museums around the world, including the National Museum in Stockholm, Sweden, and the Museum of Arts and Design in New York City. He lives in Washington state.

Wall Composition: All about Order | 2005 ▶
Collaboration with Louis Mueller
32 x 32 x 3 inches (81.3 x 81.3 x 7.6 cm)
Blown glass, spirals, powder-coated bronze
Photo by Spike Mafford

▲ **Interior Fold: Cobalt** | 2009

    24 inches (61 cm) in diameter
Blown glass, black spiral wrap

Photo by Russell Johnson

"I take advantage
of the opacity,
translucency, and
transparency of glass
in my work. I use
these characteristics
to create different
impressions in
different pieces."

▲ **Chandelier: Two Shades of White** | 2003

Collaboration with Louis Mueller
41 x 32 x 32 inches (104.1 x 81.3 x 81.3 cm)
Blown glass, white and black spiral wrap, powder-coated bronze
Photo by Russell Johnson

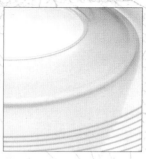

◀ **Interior Fold: White** | 2009

25 inches (63.5 cm) in diameter
Blown glass, black spiral wrap
Photos by Russell Johnson

▲ **Interior Fold Set: Manganese with Lapis Spiral Wrap** | 1996

Bowl: 22 inches (55.9 cm) in diameter
Vase: 10 x 14 inches (25.4 x 35.6 cm)
Blown glass
Photo by Russell Johnson

Interior Fold Set: Straw Colored with Blue Spiral Wrap | 1996 ▶

Bowl: 25 inches (63.5 cm) in diameter
Vase: 9 x 13 inches (22.9 x 33 cm)
Blown glass
Photo by Rob Vinnedge

◀ Interior Fold: Amethyst and Aqua | 1996

Largest: 20 inches (50.8 cm) in diameter
Blown glass, black spiral wrap
Photo by Rob Vinnedge

"For me, the true challenge of creating a piece is to instill it with a quality of timelessness. To achieve this quality, I focus on form, proportion, color, and the ways in which light interacts with the finished piece."

BENJAMIN P. MOORE

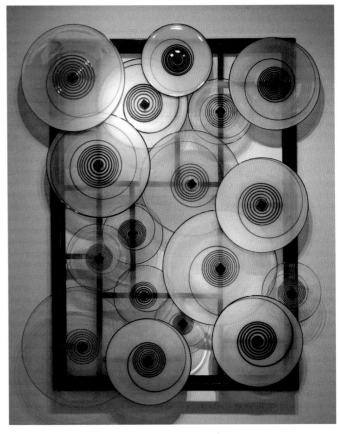

▲ **Wall Composition: Chicago** | 2005

Collaboration with Louis Mueller
48 x 60 x 3 inches (121.9 x 152.4 x 7.6 cm)
Blown glass, spiral wraps, powder-coated bronze
Photo by Spike Mafford

▲ **Wall Composition: Amsterdam** | 2005

Collaboration with Louis Mueller
48 x 60 x 3 inches (121.9 x 152.4 x 7.6 cm)
Blown glass, black spiral wraps, powder-coated bronze
Photo by Spike Mafford

"I reference simple geometric shapes, such as the sphere and cylinder, in my work. I use

color to attract attention to contour but otherwise employ very little surface decoration,

because I don't want anything to diminish the purity of the object's form."

▲ **Palla Set: Crimson** | 2009

  Bowl: 18 inches (45.7 cm) in diameter
  Vase: 18 x 5 inches (45.7 x 12.7 cm)
  Blown glass
  Photo by Russell Johnson

◀ **Palla Set: Black** | 2009

  Bowl: 17 inches (43.2 cm) in diameter
  Vase: 17 x 5 inches (43.2 x 12.7 cm)
  Blown glass
  Photos by Russell Johnson

Mark Matthews

KNOWN FOR HIS SPECTACULAR COLOR COMBINATIONS and technical virtuosity, Ohio artist Mark Matthews uses the sphere form to explore different modes of design and historical glass techniques. His remarkable sphere groupings play off of the natural-history collections that were popular during the 19th century, when carefully preserved specimens were stored in blown glass jars. Each of Matthews' marbles is a masterpiece in itself, featuring complex *filigrana*, which he manipulates with mathematical precision to create dense, complex swirls of color.

To accurately recreate the patterns of exotic animal pelts in his work, Matthews photographs examples in museums and uses the graal technique to reproduce the animals' intricate coloration. His "air traps"—the precise design elements blown and held as air in the glass—are wonderfully imaginative. Easy to get lost in, his spheres awaken a timeless sense of wonder in the viewer. Matthews' work is in the collections of the Victoria and Albert Museum in London, the Corning Museum of Glass in Corning, New York, and the National Museum of American Art in Washington, D.C., as well as many other museums around the world.

Population Portrait IX Marble Jar AP | 1995 ▶
37 x 15⅜ x 15⅜ inches (94 x 39.1 x 39.1 cm)
Blown glass, granite, iridescents; graal, filigrana,
precision-air entrapment, overlaid, zanfirico,
acid-etched
Photo by Jim King

▲ **Atomic Age and Nuclear Proliferation** | 2008

Nuclear Proliferation (top): 2 inches (5 cm) in diameter
Atomic Age (bottom): 4 inches (10.1 cm) in diameter
Glass; furnace worked, graal
Photo by artist

▲ **Super Jetson III and Two Regular Jetsons** │ 2007

Largest: 3⅛ inches (7.9 cm) in diameter
Uranium glass; furnace worked,
steam-blown air trapped

Photo by artist

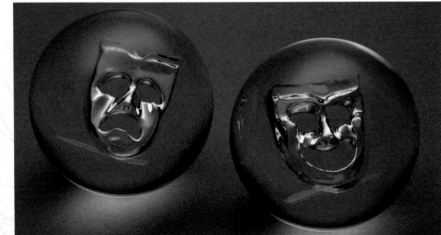

Tragedy and Comedy │ 2007 ▶

Each: 1⅞ inches (4.8 cm) in diameter
Clear glass; furnace worked,
precision-air entrapment

Photo by artist

Acid Group | 2002 ▶

7 inches (17.8 cm) in diameter
Steam-blown glass; cut, polished,
zanfirico, overlaid
Photo by Jim King

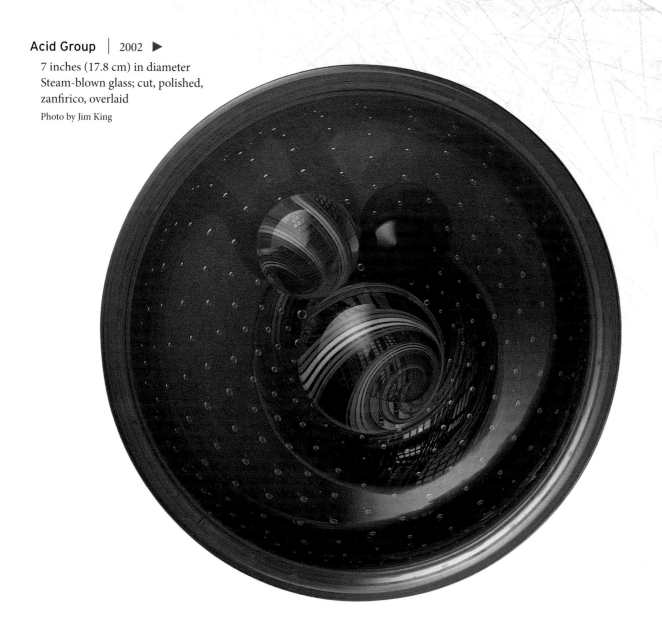

"Sphericalness is the one factor that unifies all of my diverse aesthetic experiments with glass over the past several decades. Being liberated by a self-imposed limitation is an odd paradox."

◀ **Nautica** | 2004
$3^{15}/_{16}$ x 8 inches (10 x 20.3 cm)
Blown glass; acid-etched, overlaid,
air twist, zanfirico
Photo by Jim King

Breakfast of Champions | 2004 ▶
8 inches (20.3 cm) in diameter
Blown glass; acid-etched, overlaid,
graal, zanfirico
Photo by Jim King

Purple Group | 2002 ▶

7 inches (5.2 x 17.8 cm) in diameter
Steam-blown glass; cut, polished,
overlaid, zanfirico

Photos by Jim King

"Properly formulated glass is an immortal material."

Caribbean Holiday | 2003 ▶

8¼ inches (10.2 x 21 cm) in diameter
Blown glass; acid-etched,
overlaid, zanfirico

Photo by Jim King

MARK MATTHEWS

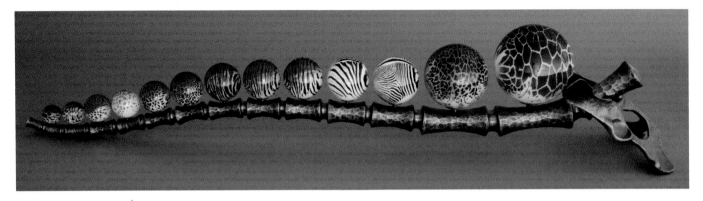

▲ Life and Death | 2006

10⅞ x 8⅝ x 51½ inches (27.6 x 21.9 x 130.8 cm)
Glass, steel; furnace worked, forged, graal
Forged steel by Joel Sanderson

Photos by artist

 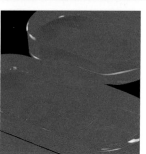

▲ **Celestial Keyboard** | 2004

52 x 38¼ x 18 inches (132.1 x 97.2 x 45.7 cm)
Glass, cherry, quilted maple, ebony,
UV light; precision-air entrapment,
cut, polished, sandblasted
Cabinet by Steve Kline

Photos by Jim King

"Extreme heat and extraordinary skill are required in order to pursue ideas in glass.

The process is both attractive and intimidating—a dichotomy I find compelling.**"**

MARK **MATTHEWS**

Preston Singletary

COMBINING EUROPEAN GLASS-BLOWING TRADITIONS with Native American iconography from the Pacific Northwest Coast, Preston Singletary draws on his Tlingit ancestry to design richly detailed, beautifully hued glass sculptures. Singletary follows a subtle, restrained aesthetic in his creation of objects that feature sacred, secular, and figurative motifs. The bowl-like Tlingit rain-hat, which has a rim that Singletary engraves with tribal patterns, is a form he returns to time and again. Inspired by the hats his ancestors made from woven cedar, his glowing glass versions are created in understated hues—shades of blue, green, and gray—and cast breathtaking shadows when they're turned upside down and a light is held over them.

   With his sharp instinct for the ways in which light can play off a piece, Singletary literally invites a spiritual element into his sculptures. By doing so, he offers a fresh approach to carrying on ancestral traditions and references the mystical realm in a personal and very contemporary manner. Based in Washington state, Singletary teaches and lectures regularly. His work is featured in museums throughout the United States and Europe.

◀ **Indian Curio Shelf** | 2009
11 x 52 x 10½ inches
(27.9 x 132.1 x 26.7 cm)
Blown glass; sand carved
Photo by Russell Johnson

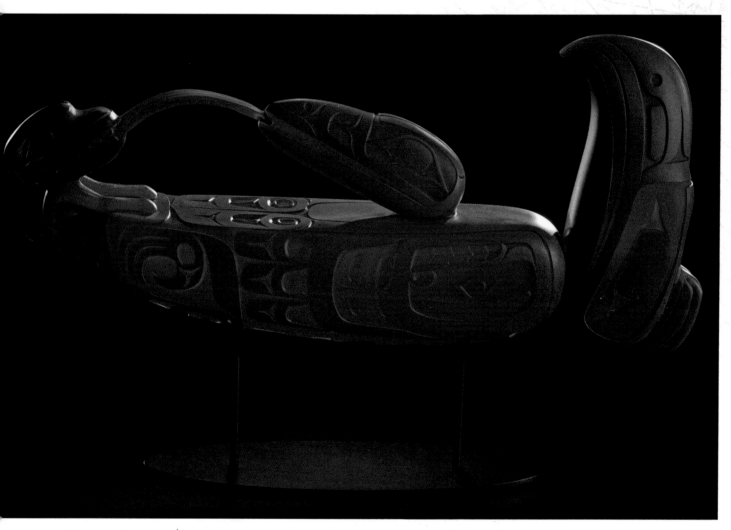

▲ Balance of Power | 2007

18 x 25 x 5 inches (45.7 x 63.5 x 12.7 cm)

Blown glass; sand carved

Photo by Russell Johnson

▼ **Spirit Canoe** | 2007
11½ x 24½ x 6½ inches (29.2 x 62.2 x 16.5 cm)
Blown glass; hot sculpted, sand carved
Photos by Russell Johnson

"I'm hoping to be able to bring Tlingit designs into the future.

Because glass is permanent, my pieces have the potential to last."

◄ **Sleeping Shaman** | 2008
25¾ x 7 x 5 inches (65.4 x 17.8 x 12.7 cm)
Blown glass; sand carved
Photo by Russell Johnson

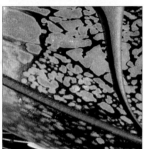

▲ **Salmon** | 2008

12 x 25 x 3½ inches (30.5 x 63.5 x 8.9 cm)
Blown glass; sand carved

Photos by Russell Johnson

▼ **Object of Curiosity** | 2008

6 x 23½ x 3½ inches
(15.2 x 59.7 x 8.9 cm)
Blown glass; sand carved

Photos by Russell Johnson

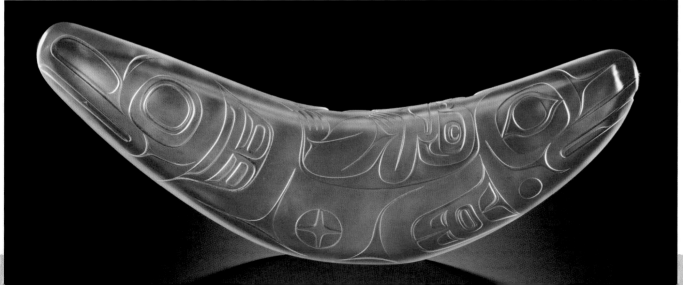

▲ **Raven Transformation Mask** | 2007

7 x 23 x 5 inches (17.8 x 58.4 x 12.7 cm)

Blown glass; sand carved

Photos by Russell Johnson

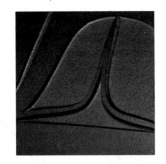

Oyster-Catcher Rattle | 2008 ▶

20 x 17 x 7½ inches
(50.8 x 43.2 x 19.1 cm)
Blown glass; hot sculpted,
sand carved

Photo by Russell Johnson

"I think of the shadows created by glass as the fourth dimension of a piece, as a kinetic sculpture that's only revealed when the lighting is right."

◀ **Spirit Rattle** | 2008
13½ x 14 x 4 inches
(34.3 x 35.6 x 10.2 cm)
Blown glass; sand carved
Photos by Russell Johnson

Beaver Hat | 2009 ▶

7½ x 18 inches
(19.1 x 45.7 cm)
Blown glass; sand carved

Photo by Russell Johnson

◀ **Killer Whale Hat** | 2007

7½ x 19 inches (19.1 x 48.3 cm)
Blown glass; sand carved

Photos by Russell Johnson

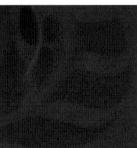

▲ **Tlingit Crest Hat** | 2009

7½ x 16¾ inches (19.1 x 42.5 cm)
Blown glass; sand carved

Photo by Russell Johnson

"My work is an extension of tradition and a declaration
that Native American cultures are alive and developing
new ways of communicating ancient symbols."

GRAY

Katherine Gray

INGENIOUSLY DESIGNED AND INSTILLED WITH a sense of playfulness, the work of Los Angeles artist Katherine Gray rarely fails to elicit a smile from the viewer. She makes everyday items seem wonderfully unfamiliar by rendering them in ways that surprise and delight. Perfectly balanced and proportioned, her cake stands flaunt conventionalism and defy functionality. This easy dismissal of traditional preciousness is part of what makes her work so amusing.

Although she creates functional objects—like flowerpots, candlesticks, and chandeliers—Gray also applies a whimsical aesthetic to these pieces, remaking them according to her personal, offbeat vision. She possesses a wonderful instinct for color, but she isn't afraid to dispense with it altogether and take advantage of glass' transparency, which shows off the ornate curves and graceful lines of her pieces to their fullest extent.

Gray's perspective-changing work can be found in the collections of the Corning Museum of Glass in Corning, New York, the Tacoma Museum of Glass in Tacoma, Washington, and the Museum of American Glass in Millville, New Jersey.

For Ever and Ever | 2005 ▶
Tallest: 16 inches (40.6 cm)
Blown glass
Photo by Victor Bracke

▲ **Tabletopiaries** | 2008

Tallest: 23 inches (58.4 cm)
Blown glass
Photo by P.J. Cybulski

▲ **Pitcher Chandelier** | 2005

25 x 28 x 28 inches (63.5 x 71.1 x 71.1 cm)
Blown glass, steel, mixed media
Photo by Victor Bracke

◄ **Candelabrum** | 1996

20 x 8 x 8 inches (50.8 x 20.3 x 20.3 cm)
Blown and hot-worked glass
Photo by Roger Schreiber

▲ **Candelabra** | 2000

Each: 18 x 12 x 6 inches
(45.7 x 30.5 x 15.2 cm)
Blown and hot-worked glass

Photo by Chris Brown Photography

"I feel that my pieces should be beautifully made and
serve multiple purposes, because there's a good chance
that they'll outlast me."

▲ **Conjoined Cake Plate III (High/Low)** | 1998

23 x 17 x 8 inches (58.4 x 43.2 x 20.3 cm)
Blown glass

Photo by Roger Schreiber

◀ **Triple-Lidded Cake Stand** | 2000

38 x 11 x 11 inches (96.5 x 27.9 x 27.9 cm)
Blown glass

Photo by Chris Brown Photography

24 x 9 x 9 inches (61 x 22.9 x 22.9 cm)
Blown glass
Photo by Chris Brown Photography

"Glass is a material that we spend a lot of time looking through, not looking at. I've invested a good part of my artistic livelihood in trying to perfect working with glass, in trying to make the invisible visible."

Russian Doll Cake Plate | 2000 ▶

25 x 9½ x 9½ inches
(63.5 x 24.1 x 24.1 cm)
Blown glass
Photo by Roger Schreiber

KATHERINE GRAY

"In my work I try to highlight the cultural significance of artisanship. I want to emphasize the value of making things in a society that's increasingly ruled by machines and simulated experiences."

▲ **Flower Pot Vases** | 2006

Each: 8 x 4 x 4 inches
(20.3 x 10.2 x 10.2 cm)
Blown and hot-worked glass

Photo by Victor Bracke

Cloudland | 2004 ▶

34 x 30 x 7 inches
(86.4 x 76.2 x 17.8 cm)
Blown glass; sandblasted

Photo by Victor Bracke

KATHERINE GRAY

◀ **Acqua Alta** | 2008
24 x 12 x 12 inches
(61 x 30.5 x 30.5 cm)
Glass, water
Photos by Victor Bracke

Maureen Williams

SOME PEOPLE SEEM TO ABSORB the very soul of the land they grew up observing. Maureen Williams is one of them. The black, white, and ocher hues featured in her compositions echo the color palette of southern Australia, where she spent her childhood. Williams uses these colors in the dynamically composed paintings that cover her blown glass vessels—paintings that explore themes of relationships and connectedness, both personal and universal, intimate and collective.

Williams is inspired by humanity's ties to the land and by the attachments, romantic and otherwise, that define our lives. Her drawings of amorphous figures and complex geometric matrices reflect these often nebulous, intermingling, and tenacious ties. The strength and quality of her lines, applied by a variety of techniques such as wheel cutting and painting, have an emotional overlay—a unique friction and intensity. Whatever their motivations—nature, emotion, or memory—her pieces stand alone as well-composed abstract works of art. Williams, who lives in St. Kilda, Australia, has participated in numerous solo and group exhibitions. Her work is owned by many institutions, including the National Gallery of Australia in Canberra, Australia, and the Die Neue Sammlung Museum in Munich, Germany.

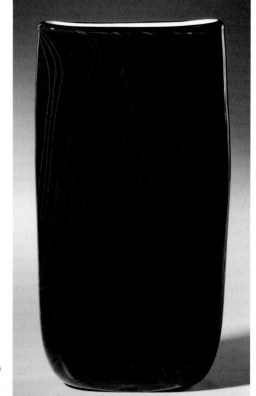

Scribbly Gum Series 1 | 2006 ▶
15¾ x 8⁷⁄₁₆ x 2¹⁵⁄₁₆ inches (40 x 21.5 x 7.5 cm)
Blown glass, paint; wheel cut, engraved
Photo by David McArthur

▲ **Larapinta Series 20** | 2006

5¹¹⁄₁₆ x 10¹³⁄₁₆ x 9⅝ inches (14.5 x 27.5 x 24.5 cm)

Blown glass, paint; wheel cut

Photo by David McArthur

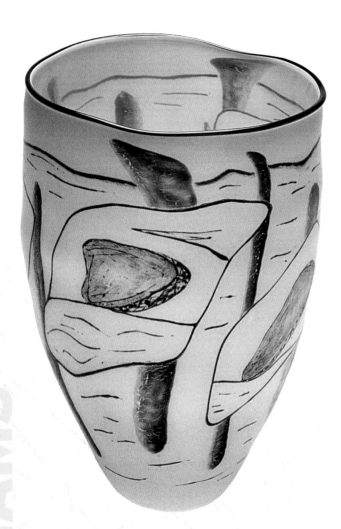

◀ **Interaction 1** │ 1997

23⅝ x 14³⁄₁₆ inches (60 x 36 cm)
Blown glass, paint
Photo by Terence Bogue

Interaction 9 │ 2000 ▶

17 x 12 inches (43 x 30 cm)
Blown glass, paint
Photo by Terence Bogue

MAUREEN WILLIAMS

▲ **Interaction 7** │ 2000

22⁷⁄₁₆ x 14¾ inches (57 x 37.5 cm)
Blown glass, paint
Photo by Peter Budd

▲ **Journeying in Parallel 9** │ 2001

13³⁄₁₆ x 8¹⁄₁₆ inches (33.5 x 20.5 cm)
Blown glass, paint; wheel cut
Photo by David McArthur

MAUREEN WILLIAMS

▲ **Larapinta Series 6** | 2004

$5^{11}/_{16}$ x $8^{5}/_{8}$ x $10^{7}/_{16}$ inches (14.5 x 22 x 26.5 cm)

Blown glass, paint; wheel cut, engraved

Photo by David McArthur

"Glass blanks shaped like eggs with color underneath serve as three-dimensional canvases for me. I draw images on these blanks, then paint them. In the blowing-up process, when the image is expanded, the painting provides a subtle background, adding dimension to the surface of the piece."

▲ Larapinta Series 1 | 2003

Largest: 6$\frac{1}{16}$ x 9$\frac{13}{16}$ x 13$\frac{3}{8}$ inches (15.5 x 25 x 34 cm)
Blown glass, paint; wheel cut
Photo by David McArthur

$18^{11}/_{16}$ x $8^{7}/_{8}$ inches (47.5 x 22.5 cm)
Blown glass, paint; wheel cut
Photo by David McArthur

▲ **Incognito 1** | 2004

$21^{7}/_{16}$ x $8^{5}/_{8}$ inches (54.5 x 22 cm)
Blown glass, paint; wheel cut
Photo by David McArthur

WILLIAMS

MAUREEN

"My imagery is often concerned with nature and civilization's imposition upon it. I use aerial views and linear aspects of land in order to comment on how man has impacted the terrain."

▲ **Obscured Landscape 4** │ 2004

18½ x 8¼ inches (47 x 21 cm)
Blown glass, paint; wheel cut

Photo by David McArthur

Altered Landscape 5 │ 2004 ▶

20¼ x 8¼ inches (51.5 x 21 cm)
Blown glass, paint; wheel cut

Photo by David McArthur

Boyd Sugiki

TRANSCENDING THE CATEGORY OF FUNCTIONAL GLASSWARE and attaining the status of sculpture, Boyd Sugiki's glasses and bottles are spirited, flamboyant, and fun. In addition to an obvious flair for contemporary design, Sugiki offers confident interpretations of contemporary patterns and architecture in his work. The pieces in his *Bottle Compositions* series are influenced by the urban landscapes he observed in Turkey. In this series, Sugiki renders towers, domes, and other structural forms prevalent in that part of the world as three-piece glass structures with crisp contours and well-proportioned curves. The clean lines and fluid arches Sugiki achieves give balance to each individual bottle and create a sense of harmony when they're grouped together.

   With their interconnected blown elements, Sugiki's precisely designed works display a modern sensibility that he has shaped into a trademark style. Sugiki lives in Washington state, and he exhibits his work in museums around the world.

◀ **Olive Martini Set** | 2000
Mixer: 10 x 6 x 6 inches
(25.4 x 15.2 x 15.2 cm)
Glasses: 6½ x 5 x 5 inches
(16.5 x 12.7 x 12.7 cm) each
Blown glass
Photo by Michael Seidl

◀ **Composition** | 2009

Tallest: 23½ x 7 x 7 inches
(59.7 x 17.8 x 17.8 cm)
Blown glass

Photo by Michael Seidl

◀ **Bottle Composition** │ 2005

53 x 9 x 9 inches
(134.6 x 22.9 x 22.9 cm)
Blown glass

Photo by Michael Seidl

Nightfall │ 2008 ▶

24½ x 9½ x 9½ inches
(62.2 x 24.1 x 24.1 cm)
Blown glass

Photo by Michael Seidl

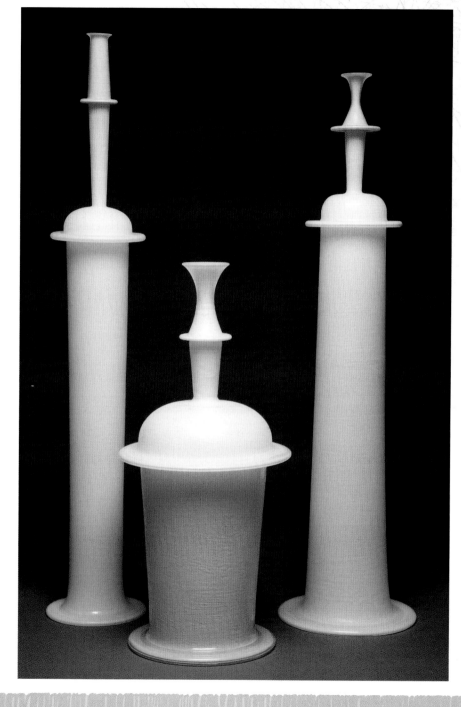

"I like to imagine that the pieces in my bottles series are towers or buildings. I believe architectural structures are containers or vessels of life, and I hope that my bottle compositions contain messages for the viewer."

◀ **Bottle Composition** │ 2005

Tallest: 41½ x 7½ x 7½ inches
(105.4 x 19.1 x 19.1 cm)
Blown glass
Photo by Michael Seidl

BOYD SUGIKI

Lemon Drop | 2003 ▶

Mixer: 16 x 6 x 6 inches
(40.6 x 15.2 x 15.2 cm)
Glasses: 6½ x 5 x 5 inches
(16.5 x 12.7 x 12.7 cm) each
Blown glass

Photo by Michael Seidl

◀ **Cordial Set** | 2006

9½ x 14 x 7½ inches
(24.1 x 35.6 x 19.1 cm)
Blown glass, steel

Photo by Michael Seidl

BOYD SUGIKI

"Balance, symmetry, and proportion are crucial elements in each of my pieces."

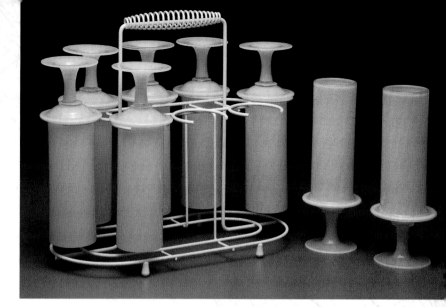

▲ **Mojito** │ 2005
12 x 14 x 7 inches (30.5 x 35.6 x 17.8 cm)
Blown glass, steel
Photo by Michael Seidl

▲ **Manhattan** │ 2003
Mixer: 12½ x 4½ x 4½ inches
(31.8 x 11.4 x 11.4 cm)
Glasses: 4½ x 3½ x 3½ inches
(11.4 x 8.9 x 8.9 cm) each
Blown glass
Photo by Michael Seidl

▲ **Highball Set** │ 2003
7 x 13 x 6 inches (17.8 x 33 x 15.2 cm)
Blown glass, steel
Photo by Michael Seidl

▲ **Striped Bowls** | 2007

Widest: 11 inches (27.9 cm) in diameter
Blown glass

Photo by Michael Seidl

▲ **Striped Bowls** │ 2007

　　Widest: 12 inches (30.5 cm) in diameter
　　Blown glass
　　Photo by Michael Seidl

"For me the development of the work is the

most fascinating part of the artistic process.

It makes me excited to go back into the

studio each day."

Josh Simpson

WHETHER THEY'RE INTERPRETED AS SCENES
from underwater or outer space, Josh Simpson's
mesmerizing works beckon the viewer to look closely at
the spectacular, miniature vistas they contain. Simpson
experiments with colorful glass canes, metal foils, trapped
air, and other techniques to produce platters and vessel
forms that are complex and enchanting.

Some of Simpson's most otherworldly sculptures were
inspired by studies of glass left over from meteorite
impacts. In these pieces Simpson pairs craggy exterior
glass surfaces with lustrous interiors, and the effect is
startlingly beautiful. His voluptuous baskets of colorless
glass blown in copper wire cages look like rock specimens
from another planet. Like the rest of Simpson's vessels
and sculptures, they have an edgy elegance.

Simpson's work is in the collections of more than
twenty major museums around the world. He lives in
Massachusetts.

▲ **Inhabited Vase** | 2004
6¾ x 5¼ x 5¼ inches (17.1 x 13.3 x 13.3 cm)
Blown glass, filigrana cane, precious metals
Photo by Tommy Olof Elder

▲ **Asymmetrical Helix** | 2008

14½ x 14½ x 1½ inches (36.8 x 36.8 x 3.8 cm)
Dark amethyst glass; latticino, hand formed and blown
Photo by Tommy Olof Elder

▼ **New Mexico Vase** │ 2004

7½ x 4½ x 4½ inches (19.1 x 11.4 x 11.4 cm)
Dark amethyst glass; hand formed and blown
Photo by Tommy Olof Elder

▲ **Galaxy Vase** │ 2006

6½ x 5½ x 1¾ inches (16.5 x 14 x 4.4 cm)
Dark amethyst glass; hand formed and blown
Photo by Lewis Legbreaker

▼ Tektite | 2004

10½ x 15¾ x 12 inches (26.7 x 40 x 7.6 cm)
New Mexico glass, meteorite glass; hand blown
Photo by Tommy Olof Elder

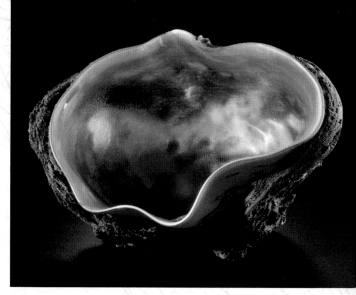

▲ Tektite | 2004

7 x 11¼ x 8½ inches
(17.8 x 28.6 x 21.6 cm)
Iridescent glass, meteorite
glass; hand blown
Photo by Tommy Olof Elder

"My motivation comes from the material itself. Glass possesses an inner light and transcendent radiant heat that makes it one of the most rewarding—and one of the most frustrating—materials to work with."

"Most of my work reflects a compromise between me and the glass. The finished piece is the moment in time when we agree."

Red New Mexico Vase | 2006 ▶

8 x 6¼ x 4¾ inches
(20.3 x 15.9 x 12.1 cm)
Dark amethyst glass; hand blown

Photo by Tommy Olof Elder

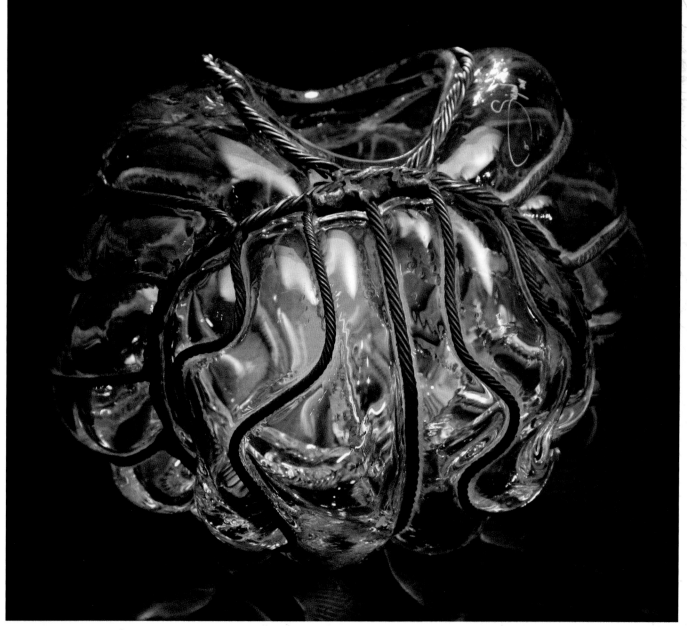

▲ Copper Basket | 2008

10 x 12 x 11½ inches (25.4 x 30.5 x 29.2 cm)
Blown glass, copper wire, patina; welded
Photo by Tim Ryan Smith

"The wonder of nature often comes out in my art—not in any purposeful way but slowly. My work evolves in such incremental steps that I often don't recognize the natural influences until someone points them out to me."

◀ **Saturn** │ 2008

Collaboration with Gabriele Küstner
15½ x 15½ x 3 inches
(39.4 x 39.4 x 7.6 cm)
Blown glass, filigrana cane,
precious metals, sculpture; incised
Photo by Tim Ryan Smith

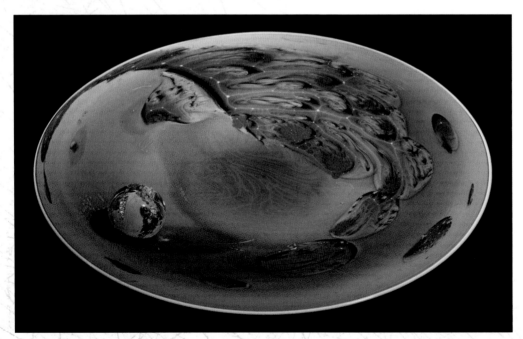

◀ **Galaxy Platter** │ 2003

16½ x 16½ x 3½ inches
(41.9 x 41.9 x 8.9 cm)
New Mexico glass, sculpture;
blown, fused
Photo by Tommy Olof Elder

◄ Corona Platter | 2009

10¼ x 10¼ x 1¼ inches
(26 x 26 x 3.2 cm)
Colloidal silver glass, crystal;
hand formed and blown, overlaid

Photo by Tim Ryan Smith

Corona Platter | 2009 ►

19½ x 19½ x 2 inches
(49.5 x 49.5 x 5.1 cm)
Colloidal silver glass, crystal;
hand formed and blown, overlaid

Photo by Tim Ryan Smith

JOSH **SIMPSON**

Richard Meitner

HIS SCULPTURES ARE UNCOMPROMISINGLY PERCEPTIVE. The work's eloquence draws on familiar forms, shrewdly bestowed with heady cultural references. Given Richard Meitner's family background in physics—his great aunt Lise Meitner helped discover nuclear fission—it's no surprise that scientific methodology and phenomena often surface in his work. And at times, irreverence provides an undercurrent.

While Meitner's studies explore avenues that absorb him, the themes have a universality that forces us to examine the sharpness of our own judgment, insight, wisdom, and understanding. It can nibble away at our psyche or any sense of complacency. Meitner is an artist whose work makes us think. The intricacies change as our experience or power of observation sharpens. There is always something else to glean.

Meitner often uses a combination of glassworking techniques and collected objects in his pieces. His work has been exhibited internationally and is included in the permanent collections of more than 50 museums worldwide. He lives in Amsterdam, the Netherlands.

My Note | 2009 ▶

29½ inches (75 cm) in height
Blown borosilicate glass, glass
lacquer, rubber stoppers; fired

Photo by Ron Zijlstra

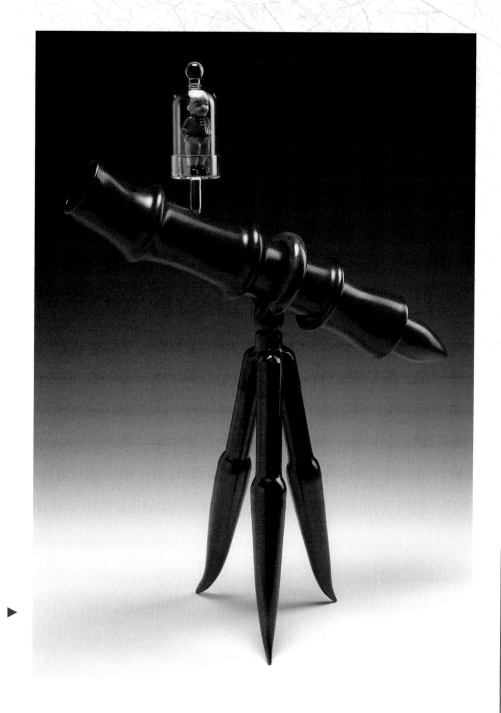

Me and Oriental Science | 2006 ▶

22 inches (56 cm) tall
Blown borosilicate glass,
porcelain figure, epoxy ring;
enamel fired, painted

Photo by Ron Zijlstra

Zanzibar 1963 | 2009 ▶

26 x 9¹⁄₁₆ x 13³⁄₈ inches
(66 x 23 x 34 cm)
Blown borosilicate glass, lacquer
paint, rubber stoppers; fired
Photos by Ron Zijlstra

◀ **Resolute** | 2009

26 x 7⅞ x 10⅝ inches (66 x 20 x 27 cm)
Blown borosilicate glass, lacquer paint, rubber stoppers; fired
Photos by Ron Zijlstra

"My many trips to antique shops have resulted in a collection of objects that appeal to me because I feel they're fragments of stories that I don't know but can sense. These items often find their way into my pieces, and so the works themselves also become stories—fragmented narratives that viewers may or may not pick up on."

"I think play should be taken very seriously."

▲ **Delfts Blue** | 1997
$19^{11}/_{16}$ x $15\frac{3}{4}$ x $11^{13}/_{16}$ inches (50 x 40 x 30 cm)
Blown glass, glass tiles, enamel; fired
Photo by Ron Zijlstra

Schroedinger's Cat | 2000 ▶

35 inches (88 cm) tall
Blown borosilicate and soda-lime glasses,
iron coating, colored water
Photo by Ron Zijlstra

▼ **My Seed . . . to Spend or Save?** | 2004

15 inches (39 cm) tall
Crystal sculpture
Photo by Ron Zijlstra

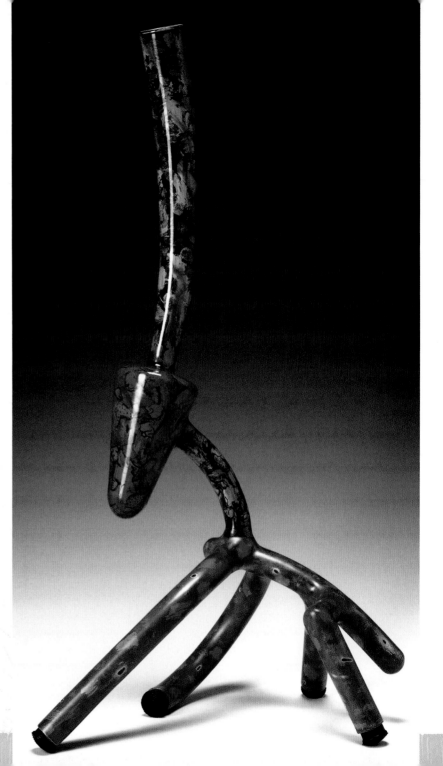

"If you blow a cylindrical vase form, then flatten the top half so that the front and back surfaces are close to each other, two transparent canvasses—one behind the other— are created. This 'playing field' has led me to many complex and interesting discoveries."

Ceramics Hystery | 2009 ▶
26 x 10¼ x 14³⁄₁₆ inches
(66 x 26 x 36 cm)
Blown borosilicate glass, lacquer
paint, rubber stoppers; fired
Photo by Ron Zijlstra

RICHARD MEITNER

◀ **Alice** | 1999

20 x 10 inches (50.8 x 25.4 cm)
Blown borosilicate glass,
found objects

Photo by Ron Zijlstra

Debora Moore

TAKING THE OBJECTIVE CONCEPT OF NATURAL HISTORY and giving it a deeply subjective interpretive overlay, Debora Moore produces works of singular splendor and originality. Her flowers are conventionally beautiful, but the viewer soon realizes that they also possess exotic hothouse eccentricities. An element of danger and darkness—an overreaching leaf, a rotting branch—dilutes each bloom's majesty. This combination of beauty and ominousness adds to the intrigue of the wild environment Moore conjures with her glass botanicals—an atmosphere that's at once oppressive and nourishing.

Moore's fanciful, vividly colored creations also serve as a reference to the obsessive fervor of orchid lovers, whose passion is driven by a need to possess those emblems of exoticism. With their opulent colors and luxurious textures, her flowers seem to hum with the energy of nature. Moore is a member of the African-American Design Archive at the Cooper-Hewitt National Design Museum in New York City. Her work has been exhibited at numerous museums and galleries, including the Smithsonian Institution in Washington, D.C., and is in the permanent collection of the Corning Museum of Glass in Corning, New York.

◀ **Spring** │ 2008
96 x 96 x 8 inches
(243.8 x 243.8 x 20.3 cm)
Blown and sculpted glass
Photos by Douglas Schaible

◄ **Host XX** | 2008

16 x 6 x 6 inches
(40.6 x 15.2 x 15.2 cm)
Blown and sculpted glass

Photo by Lynn Thompson

Bamboo Grove | 2005 ▶

154 x 76 x 20 inches
(391.2 x 193 x 50.8 cm)
Blown and sculpted glass

Photos by Russell Johnson

▲ **Phalaenopsis: Wall Sculpture** | 2002

24 x 13 x 8 inches (61 x 33 x 20.3 cm)
Blown and sculpted glass
Photo by Lynn Thompson

"Glass' ability to transmit and reflect light, as well
as its variations from transparency to opacity,
make it especially appealing to me as a medium."

▲ **Brassia Spider Orchid Leaf** | 2002

16½ x 12 x 7 inches (41.9 x 30.5 x 17.8 cm)
Blown and sculpted glass
Photo by Lynn Thompson

▲ **Host XXII** | 2008
21 x 13 x 10 inches (53.3 x 33 x 25.4 cm)
Blown and sculpted glass
Photo by Lynn Thompson

▲ **Host V: Purple Epidendrum** | 2006
25 x 12 x 11 inches (63.5 x 30.5 x 27.9 cm)
Blown and sculpted glass
Photo by Spike Mafford

"I enjoy starting out with something that's inherently 'glassy' and transforming it into a piece that's organic and natural."

▲ **Blue Epiphyte** | 2008

22 x 9½ x 7½ inches
(55.9 x 24.1 x 19.1 cm)
Blown and sculpted glass

Photo by Lynn Thompson

▲ **Tree Series: Yellow Lady Slipper** | 2008

25½ x 13 x 12 inches (64.8 x 33 x 30.5 cm)
Blown and sculpted glass

Photo by Lynn Thompson

▲ **Host I: Pink and Green Epidendrum** | 2006

21 x 7½ x 8½ inches (53.3 x 19.1 x 21.6 cm)
Blown and sculpted glass

Photo by Spike Mafford

◀ **Tree Series: Brassia Orchid** │ 2008

65 x 32 x 11 inches
(165.1 x 81.3 x 27.9 cm)
Blown and sculpted glass
Photos by Lynn Thompson

"The delicacy and
inherent properties
of glass have helped
me cultivate an
organic approach
to sculpture."

DEBORA MOORE

Marvin Lipofsky

WITH THEIR BOLD FIELDS OF COLOR AND SENSUOUS CURVES, Marvin Lipofsky's deconstructed, vessel-like bubbles show off the sculptural dimensions and rich textural qualities of glass. Fluid and wavy, airy and light, the pieces resemble seashells or some new organic life form. They fold in on themselves as if to retain the artist's breath, and yet they open invitingly to expose the secrets of their interiors. Lipofsky cuts, hand shapes, sandblasts, and acid polishes these pieces to produce a contrast between the inner and outer surfaces. Several of his series work off this sort of textural tension. Lipofsky often establishes this juxtaposition through the pairing of a matte exterior with a luminous interior.

Visually stunning, the colorful exuberance of Lipofsky's works reflect his passion for nature and desire to capture its rhythms. Lipofsky, who lives in Berkeley, California, has work in more than 100 collections around the world, including the Metropolitan Museum of Art in New York City, the Philadelphia Museum of Art in Philadelphia, and the National Museum of Modern Art in Kyoto, Japan.

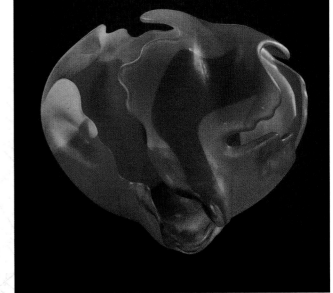

Bezalel Group 2005 #2 | 2005 ▶
11 x 14 x 13 inches (27.9 x 35.6 x 33 cm)
Blown glass; cut, sandblasted, acid-polished
Photo by M. Lee Fatherree

▲ **Russian Group 2006-2007 #7** | 2006–2007

    11 x 18 x 14 inches (27.9 x 45.7 x 35.6 cm)

    Blown glass; cut, sandblasted, acid-polished

    Photo by M. Lee Fatherree

"My forms are pretty much the same, yet they're always different. If you look at the work in one of my series, you'll see that the pieces have a general context, but they're all varied.**"**

▲ **The 4 Seasons–I Quattro Stagioni** │ 1998

42 x 48 x 48 inches
(106.7 x 121.9 x 121.9 cm)
Blown glass, charcoal drawing;
cut, sandblasted, acid-polished
Photo by M. Lee Fatherree

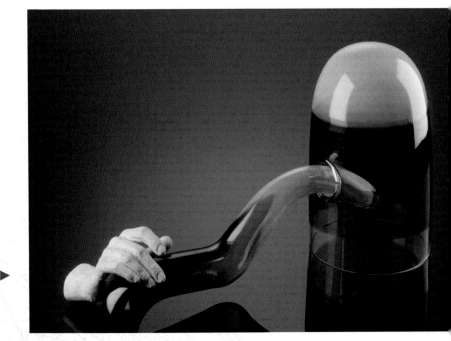

Lerrdam Color Series 1970 LT12 │ 1970 ▶

12½ x 26 x 8¼ inches (31.8 x 66 x 21 cm)
Blown glass, ceramic
Photo by M. Lee Fatherree

◀ **California Loop Series** | 1968

14½ x 27½ x 7½ inches
(36.8 x 69.9 x 19.1 cm)
Blown glass, paint, rayon flocking,
mixed media

Photo by M. Lee Fatherree

Nanbu Group 1975 #4 | 1975 ▶

7¼ x 17 x 9 inches
(18.4 x 43.2 x 22.9 cm)
Blown glass

Photo by M. Lee Fatherree

MARVIN **LIPOFSKY**

▲ **Fratelli-Toso 1976-78** | 1976–1978

13 x 28 inches (33 x 71.1 cm)

Blown glass

Photo by M. Lee Fatherree

▼ **IGS II 1985-93 #4** | 1985–1993

14½ x 22½ x 17½ inches (36.8 x 57.2 x 44.5 cm)

Blown glass; cut, sandblasted, acid-polished

Photo by M. Lee Fatherree

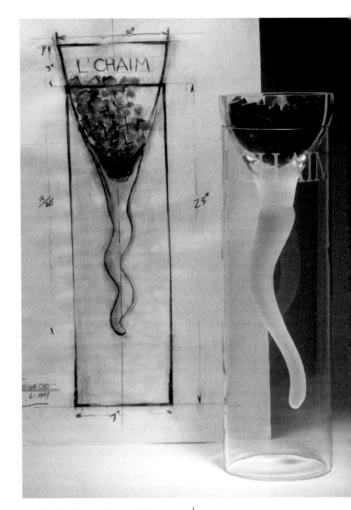

▲ **A Kiddush Cup: L'Chaim** | 1997

25 x 7½ inches (63.5 x 19.1 cm)

Blown glass; cut, sandblasted, acid-polished

Photo by M. Lee Fatherree

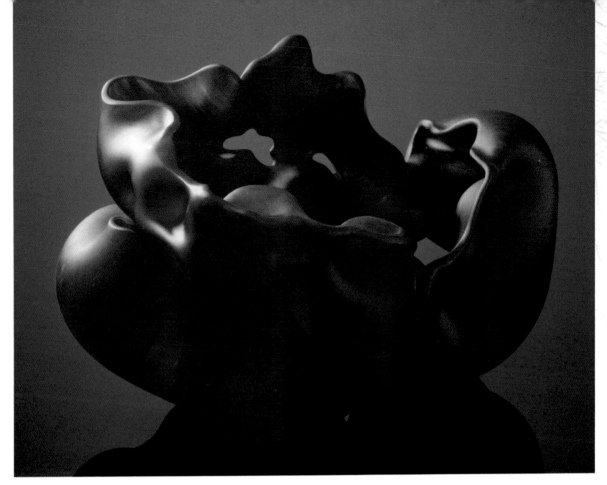

▲ **China Group II 1999-2000 #10** | 1999–2000

10 x 15 x 13½ inches (25.4 x 38.1 x 34.3 cm)
Blown glass; cut, sandblasted, acid-polished
Photo by M. Lee Fatherree

"Travel provides inspiration for many of my pieces. With my *China* series, for example, I tried to recreate the feel of the mountains in that country, because they're so different from other mountains I've seen. I also incorporated small bits of color into each piece to represent the many different peoples of that nation."

▲ IGS VII 2000-2002 #8 | 2000–2002
14 x 18½ x 20 inches (35.6 x 47 x 50.8 cm)
Blown glass; cut, sandblasted, acid-polished
Photo by M. Lee Fatherree

▲ Czech Flowers 1991-93 #10 | 1991–1993
11 x 17 inches (27.9 x 43.2 cm)
Blown glass; cut, sandblasted, acid-polished
Photo by M. Lee Fatherree

"My process is primarily intuitive. I don't think in advance about what I'm going to do.

I prefer to let an idea or a work situation develop naturally."

▼ L'viv Group 2001-2002 #2 | 2001–2002

8½ x 18½ x 18 inches (21.6 x 47 x 45.7 cm)
Blown glass; cut, sandblasted, acid-polished
Photo by M. Lee Fatherree

Dick Weiss

IN THE WONDERFULLY INSTINCTIVE CARICATURES and portraits that he executes on glass vessels, Dick Weiss creates very personal renderings—depictions that offer rich insights into the temperaments of each of his subjects. Weiss often does self-portraits, some comic, others deeply poignant and emotive in their chronicling of his personal evolution. The base, the sometimes flared opening, and other details, such as unusual prunts or knobs, all work together to guide the overall shape of each piece and reinforce the fundamental image Weiss has chosen to portray.

Weiss' use of color is always perceptive—a rich indulgence that allows him to capture precise human traits the viewer immediately recognizes and connects with. In their presentation of the core of each character, his portraits have an honesty that is both refreshing and instructive. Bringing to mind the proverbial genie in a bottle, his paintings seem to summon a magical internal force—a spirit sequestered within the vessel. Weiss' work is in the permanent collections of the Victoria and Albert Museum in London, the Corning Museum in Corning, New York, and the Glasmuseum in Frauenau, Germany. He lives in Seattle, Washington, with his wife, artist Sonja Blomdahl.

Portrait of a Woman | 2004 ▶

16 x 9 x 5 inches (40.6 x 22.9 x 12.7 cm)
Blown glass; painted

Blank blown by Dante Marioni
Photo by artist

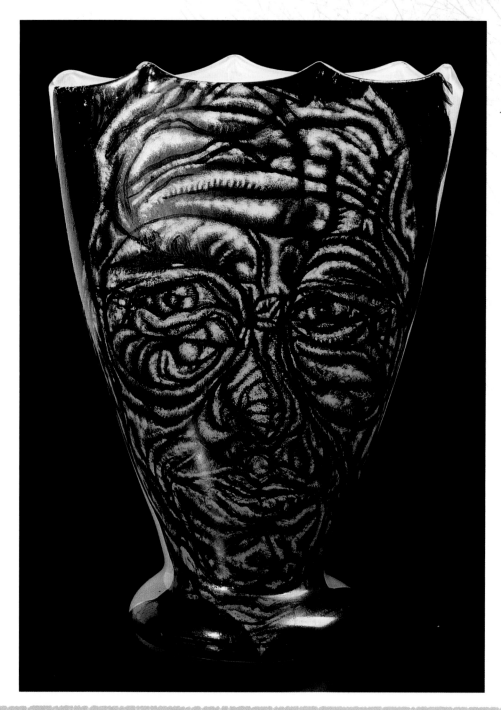

◀ **Self-Portrait with Lines** | 2007

22 x 14 x 6 inches
(55.9 x 35.6 x 15.2 cm)
Blown glass, enamels

Blank blown by Benjamin Moore
Photo by Roger Schreiber

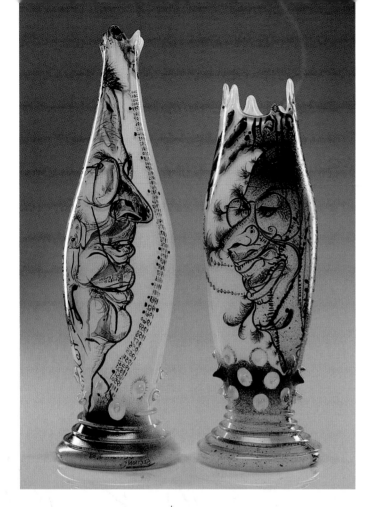

▲ **Self-Portrait Vessels** | 2003–2006

Left: 23 x 7 x 7 inches (58.4 x 17.8 x 17.8 cm)
Right: 20 x 6 x 6 inches (50.8 x 15.2 x 15.2 cm)
Blown glass; painted

Blanks blown by Dante Marioni
Photo by Dick Marquis

Self-Portrait Vessel | 2004 ▶

21 x 7 x 7 inches (53.3 x 17.8 x 17.8 cm)
Blown glass; painted

Vessel blank blown by Dante Marioni
Photo by Dick Marquis

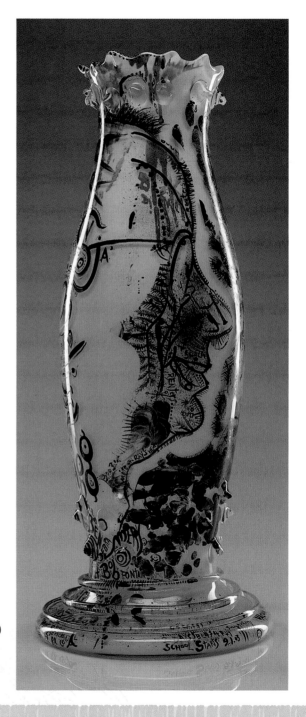

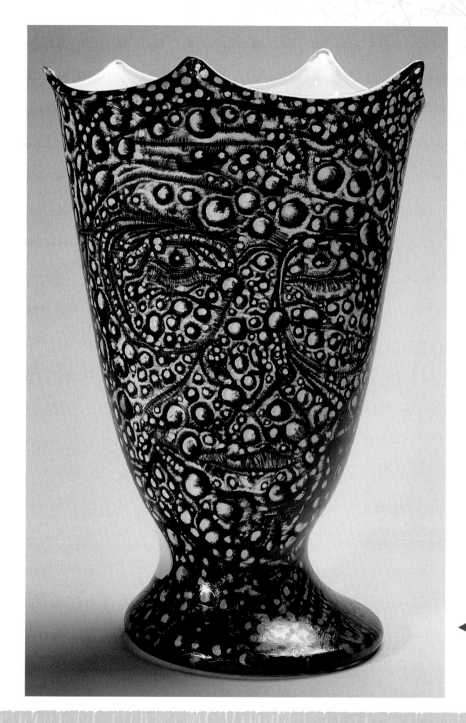

"Paint is a wonderful medium when joined with hand-blown glass."

◀ **Man with Dots** │ 2005

23 x 11 x 6 inches (58.4 x 27.9 x 15.2 cm)
Blown glass; painted

Blank blown by Benjamin Moore
Photo by artist

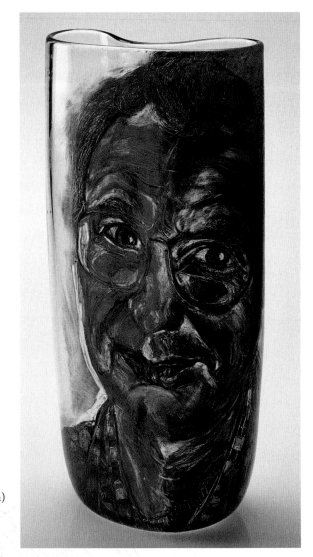

◀ **Portrait of Brother Dave** | 2003

25 x 11 x 6 inches (63.5 x 27.9 x 15.2 cm)
Blown glass; painted

Vessel blown by Benjamin Moore
Photo by Roger Schreiber

Self-Portrait | 2006 ▶

24 x 11 x 5 inches (61 x 27.9 x 12.7 cm)
Blown glass; painted

Blank blown by Janusz Pozniak
Photo by Roger Schreiber

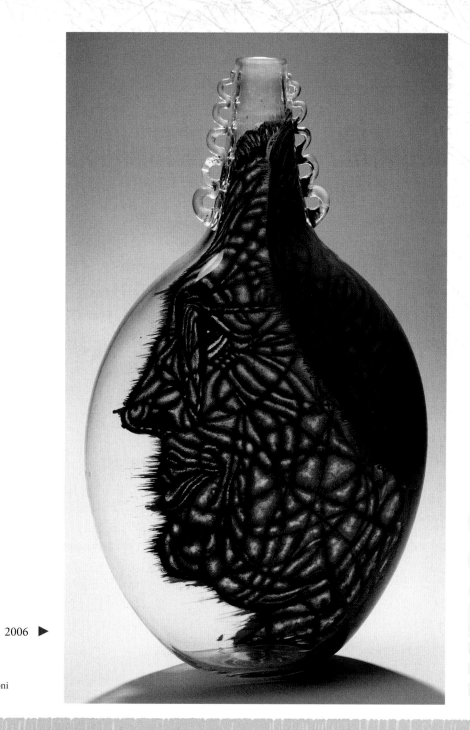

"My glass-blowing friends showed me the value of a bottle. I came to see how special the vessel is, how magical."

Face with Lines: Martinuzzi Handles | 2006 ▶

23 x 13 x 5 inches (58.4 x 33 x 12.7 cm)
Blown glass; painted

Vessel blank blown by Benjamin Moore and Dante Marioni
Photo by Roger Schreiber

▼ **Portrait of Fritz Dreisbach** | 2006

17 x 7 x 7 inches (43.2 x 17.8 x 17.8 cm)

Blown glass; painted

Blank blown by Fritz Dreisbach
Photo by Roger Schreiber

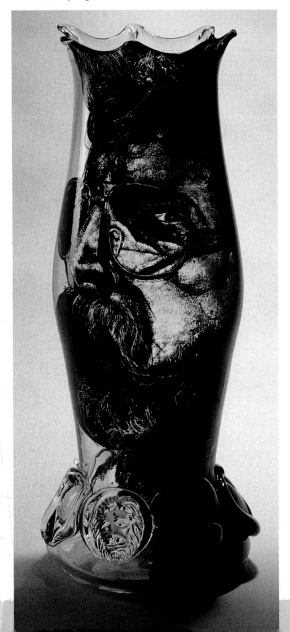

▲ **Portrait of John Landon** | 2006

22 x 13 x 13 inches (55.9 x 33 x 33 cm)

Blown glass, enamel

Blank blown by Benjamin Moore
Photo by Roger Schreiber

"It only took me 20 years to realize my friends could blow me things I could paint on."

▲ **Portrait of a Man** | 2007

23 x 7 x 7 inches (58.4 x 17.8 x 17.8 cm)
Blown glass; painted

Blank blown by Dante Marioni
Photo by Russell Johnson

▲ **Portrait of Cappy Thompson** | 2006

22 x 14 x 6 inches (55.9 x 35.6 x 15.2 cm)
Blown glass; painted

Blank blown by Benjamin Moore
Photo by Russell Johnson

DICK WEISS

Joel Philip Myers

IN WORK THAT CELEBRATES THE FULL POTENTIAL OF COLOR—its ability to serve as an accent or an exclamation, to bring subtle nuance or strong emphasis to a piece—Joel Philip Myers demonstrates an intense awareness of the intimate relationship between color and shape. Myers' vessels possess unique depth and density thanks to their multiple layers of glass and the glass bits that he adds while blowing. From vividly hued cylinders to stark, conceptual sculptures, he has long explored different forms, departing from the orthodox vessel shape for experiments in both representation and abstraction.

With some vessels, Myers reconfigures the traditional bottle motif, so that each segment of the piece seems to mimic body language. When grouped together, the textures, colors, and patterns of these vessels have a heightened effect. Each piece is distinct, yet each contributes to the general grandeur of Myers' concept.

His work is featured in numerous collections internationally, including those of the Art Institute of Chicago in Chicago, the Metropolitan Museum of Art in New York City, and the Musée Des Arts Décoratifs in Paris. Myers lives in Marietta, Pennsylvania, and Copenhagen, Denmark.

Dialogue #5 | 1999 ▶
Tallest: 15 x 4½ inches
(38.1 x 11.4 cm)
Mold-blown glass
Photo by John Herr

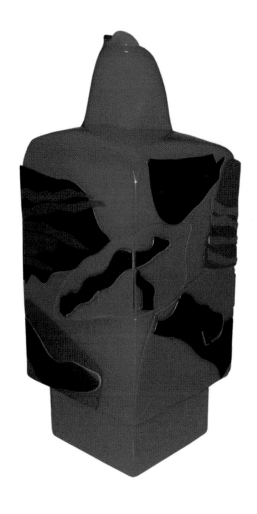

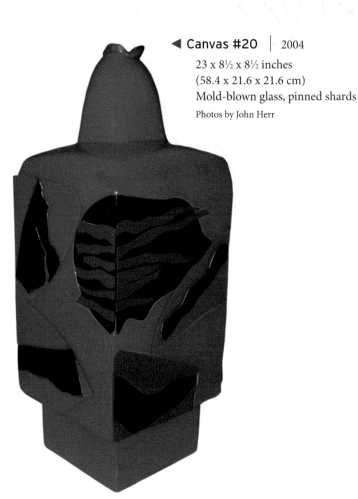

◀ **Canvas #20** │ 2004

23 x 8½ x 8½ inches
(58.4 x 21.6 x 21.6 cm)
Mold-blown glass, pinned shards

Photos by John Herr

▼ White Fish │ 1991

31½ x 8⁵⁄₁₆ x 3⁷⁄₁₆ inches (80 x 21.2 x 8.7 cm)
Blown glass, shard additions, cane additions
Photo by Douglas Schaible

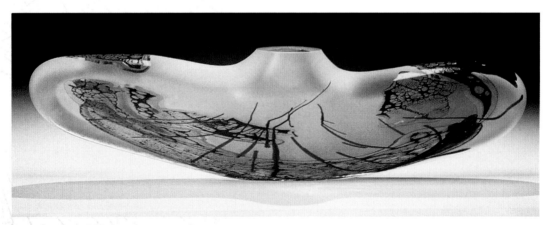

▲ Laisel V │ 1985

27 x 6⅞ x 3 inches (68.5 x 17.4 x 7.8 cm)
Blown glass, shard additions, cane additions
Photo by Douglas Schaible

"The flattened, spherical form is my format of choice because it represents for me the most perfect, eternal, universal true form. The spherical form serves but does not itself dominate the images reflected in it and through it."

▲ Kaleidoscope III | 1990

16¼ x 14½ x 3½ inches (41.3 x 36.8 x 8.9 cm)
Blown glass, shard additions
Photos by Douglas Schaible

"I work with simple forms and concentrate on surface enrichment. I prefer a three-dimensional surface to a flat one, because as I paint and draw on the glass, the glass form receives the drawing, adapts to its shape, distorts, and expands it.**"**

▲ **Valmuen IV** | 1990

15 x 14⅝ x 3¹³⁄₁₆ inches
(38.1 x 37.1 x 9.7 cm)
Blown glass, shard additions

Photos by Douglas Schaible

JOEL PHILIP

▼ Facet Red | 1987

11½ x 9¼ x 3 inches (29.2 x 23.5 x 7.6 cm)
Blown glass, shard additions; cut, polished

Photos by Douglas Schaible

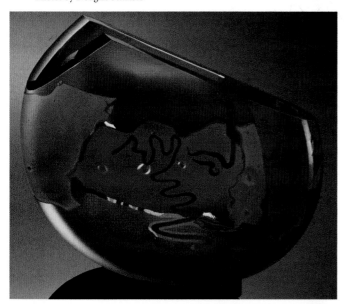

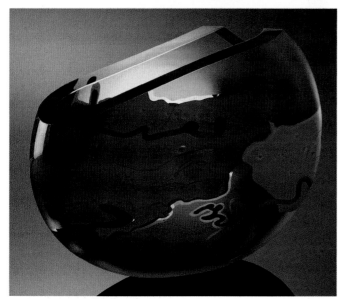

▲ Homage | 1991

14½ x 16 x 4 inches (36.8 x 40.6 x 10.2 cm)
Blown glass, shard additions

Photos by Douglas Schaible

6⅞ x 3¾ inches
(17.5 x 9.5 cm)
Blown glass; sandblasted,
acid-etched

Photos by artist

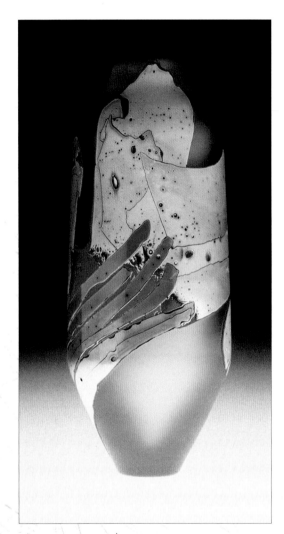

▲ **CFCBJG 59** | 1981

11¾ x 5 inches (29.8 x 12.7 cm)
Blown glass; surface tooled, acid-etched,
sandblasted

Photo by artist

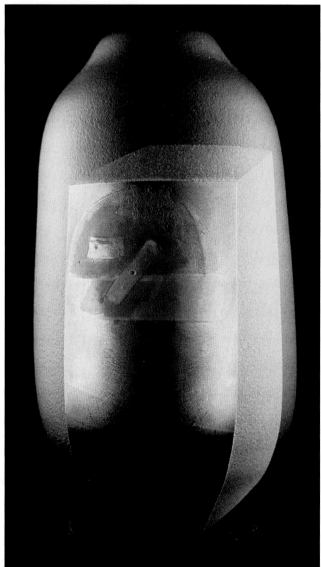

▲ **Color Study #14** | 2001

22 x 5½ inches
(55.9 x 14 cm)
Mold-blown glass
Photo by John Herr

▲ **The Ghosts of War** | 1997

Tallest: 22 x 5½ inches (55.9 x 14 cm)
Mold-blown glass; hand manipulated
Photo by Ron Zijlstra

"As an artist I like to think of myself as a visitor in a maze,
trying to find a solution to a dizzying puzzle. As in a maze,
through blunders and exploration I have arrived at solutions
and now embrace the manifold possibilities my material
offers: plasticity, transparency, opacity, translucency.**"**

JOEL PHILIP MYERS

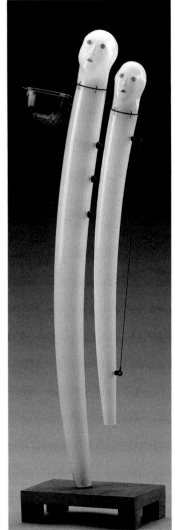

Joey Kirkpatrick & Flora Mace

OVER THE COURSE OF A THIRTY-ONE-YEAR COLLABORATION
that began when they met at Stanwood, Washington's Pilchuck Glass School, Flora
Mace and Joey Kirkpatrick have produced an innovative body of work that includes
glass vessels with applied imagery and sculptures created from glass, wood, and
other media. Using Kirkpatrick's natural history drawings as a foundation, the pair
creates clear vessels with cast panels that mimic bird identification books. To make
fine details such as bird feathers in these pieces, Kirkpatrick layers powdered colored
glasses on a metal plate, then pours molten glass into a form surrounding the image.
The powdered colors and liquid glass fuse as a "page" resembling an entry from a
local guidebook.

Mace and Kirkpatrick also create fanciful oversized forms—fruits and pots of paint
made by using twisted colored canes. The enlarged pieces are evidence of the perfect
control the two have achieved in their chosen medium. Their collaborative work is
in galleries around the world, including the Metropolitan Museum of Art in New
York City, the Musée des Arts Décoratifs in Lausanne,
Switzerland, and the Smithsonian American Art
Museum in Washington, D.C.

Foregather | 1985 ▶
32 x 10 x 5 inches (81.3 x 25.4 x 12.7 cm)
Blown glass, enamel, wire, slate;
off hand and mold blown, fabricated
Photos by Robert Vinnedge

▲ **Animal Alphabet: A, B, C, D, E** | 2009

    Largest: 6½ x 5¼ x 5¼ inches (16.5 x 13.3 x 13.3 cm)

    Blown glass; glass-powder drawing

    Photo by Robert Vinnedge

▲ **Zanfirico Still Life** | 1996
Pear: 25 x 15 x 16 inches (63.5 x 38.1 x 40.6 cm)
Blown glass, crushed glass powders; blown overlay
Photo by Robert Vinnedge

"We like to work with everyday, commonplace objects. By using these forms, which are to us innately beautiful, we both embrace tradition and distinguish ourselves within it."

▲ Still Life with Purple Plum | 2000

29 x 49 x 49 inches (73.7 x 124.5 x 124.5 cm)
Blown glass, glass powders, wood; hand carved
Photo by Robert Vinnedge

▼ Fruit and Vegetable Goblet Wall | 1999

50 x 30 x 7 inches (127 x 76.2 x 17.8 cm)
Blown glass, crushed glass powders
Photo by Robert Vinnedge

▲ **Bird Page Installation** | 2005

Installation: 17½ x 60 x 12 inches (44.5 x 152.4 x 30.5 cm)
Blown glass, steel; off-hand blown, glass-powder drawing

Photos by Robert Vinnedge

▼ Backyard Birds: First Facts | 2002

32 x 38 x 10 inches
(81.3 x 96.5 x 25.4 cm)
Blown glass; glass-powder drawing

Photo by Robert Vinnedge

"Our experiences with two-dimensional painting led to the process we use now for making still lifes. We build layers of color by sifting colored, crushed glass onto the hot glass during the blowing process. This method of painting in three dimensions was an exciting discovery for us."

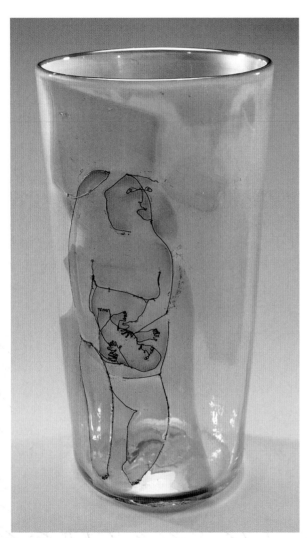

▲ **Babies and Baskets Are Not Strangers** | 1980

11½ x 6 x 6 inches (29.2 x 15.2 x 15.2 cm)
Blown glass; wire drawing
Photo by Claire Garoutte

▼ **Nippon Doll II** | 1982

11 x 7½ x 7½ inches (27.9 x 19.1 x 19.1 cm)
Blown glass; wire and glass-thread drawing
Photo by Claire Garoutte

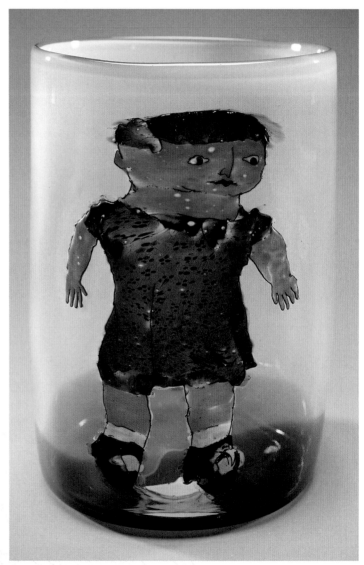

"Collaborating is sometimes difficult, but we find that the scrutiny of two artists helps us to better identify what's unnecessary in a piece."

▲ **Paintbrush Group: Making before Meaning** | 2007
Installation: 77 x 40 x 40 inches (195.6 x 101.6 x 101.6 cm)
Blown glass, wood, fiber, steel; fabricated
Photo by Robert Vinnedge

Daniel Spitzer

INSPIRED BY THE IDEA THAT ON FIRST VIEWING a work of art can be open to interpretation, Daniel Spitzer creates pieces that invite viewers to look closely and think deeply. Always lively and surprising, his vessels and sculptures reveal his dry sense of humor and willingness to experiment. Spitzer's chandeliers are delightfully offbeat and fluidly designed. Working with a multiplicity of elements, including the charcoal drawings that are frequently used as backdrops to his glass pieces, he employs a variety of media to create provocative art.

Spitzer often works in monotones, which allow viewers to clearly observe form and composition. The use of monotones also makes it possible for him to strip a concept down to its essence and highlight the tension between the segments of a piece. His work has purity and elegance.

Spitzer, who lives in Beacon, New York, has taught both nationally and internationally. In addition to his own work, he has created pieces for many non-glassworking artists, including a series of full-size blown-glass car tires for Robert Rauschenberg.

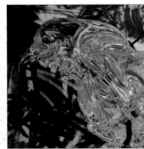

Glass Gesture 3 | 2008 ▶
30½ x 17 x 12½ inches
(77.5 x 43.2 x 31.8 cm)
Sculpted glass, wood, paper, brass, charcoal
Photos by artist

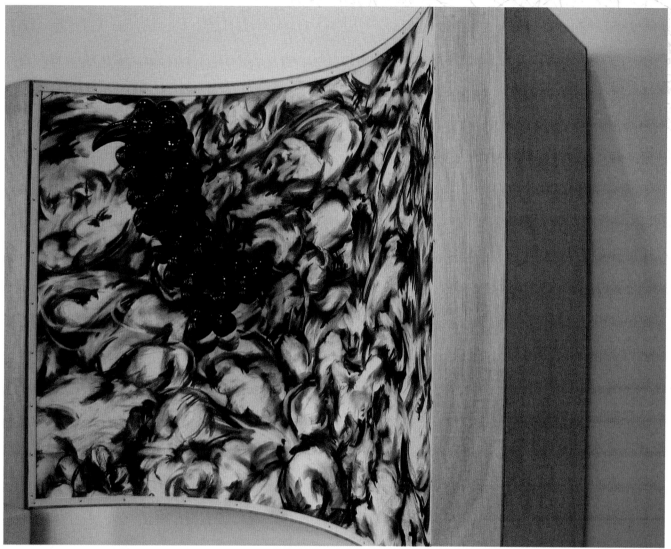

▲ **Glass Gesture 2** | 2008

22½ x 30 x 10 inches (57.2 x 76.2 x 25.4 cm)
Sculpted glass, wood, paper, brass, charcoal

Photos by artist

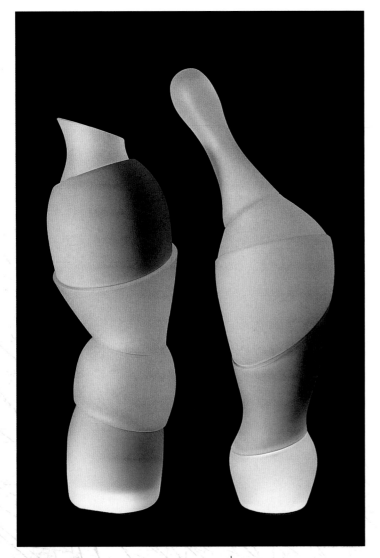

▲ **Reconstruction: Clear and Grey** | 2000

16½ x 11 x 5 inches (41.9 x 27.9 x 12.7 cm)
Blown glass; cut, sandblasted, glued
Photo by artist

▲ **Reconstruction: Clear and Purple** | 2000

19 x 6 inches (48.3 x 15.2 cm)
Blown glass; cut, sandblasted, glued
Photo by artist

DANIEL SPITZER

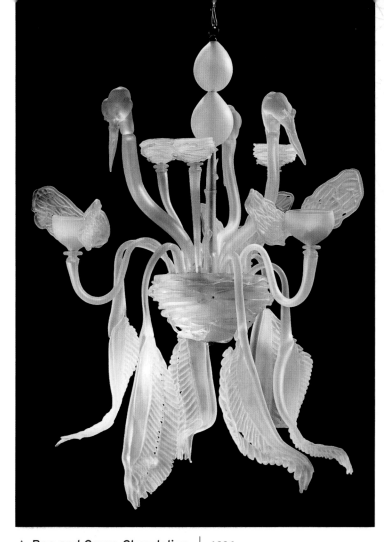

▲ Bee and Crane Chandelier │ 1996

   45 x 38 inches (114.3 x 96.5 cm)
   Blown and sculpted glass, steel; sandblasted
   Photo by artist

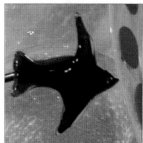

▲ Dust Up │ 2005

   66 x 48 inches (167.6 x 121.9 cm)
   Blown and sculpted glass, steel
   Photos by John Beale

"I'm always looking for ways to combine my love of pictorial representation with my skills

as a glassblower and sculptor."

DANIEL SPITZER

"In order to diminish the distinction between glass sculpting and drawing, I often layer repeated glass elements as I work. Just as marks on paper combine to form a drawing, these repeated glass elements combine to form a gestural object."

▲ Cadmium Red Teapot with Orange Spouts | 1995
11 x 11 inches (27.9 x 27.9 cm)
Blown glass
Photo by Claire Garoutte

▲ Lapis Teapot with Royal Blue Spouts │ 1996

    16 x 11 inches (40.6 x 27.9 cm)
    Blown glass
    Photo by Claire Garoutte

▲ Can You Say Shrew? │ 2003

    8 x 6 x 4 inches (20.3 x 15.2 x 10.2 cm)
    Sculpted glass
    Photo by artist

DANIEL SPITZER

◀ **Murrini Vase** | 1995
16 x 8 inches (40.6 x 20.3 cm)
Blown glass; murrini pick-up
Photos by Claire Garoutte

"I'm interested in the slippage that occurs between thought and expression. This slippage inspires me to create visual metaphors—pieces that explore the unstable ground between seeing, comprehension, and representation."

◀ **Reconstruction: Amber** | 2000

14 x 7 inches (35.6 x 17.8 cm)
Blown glass; cut, sandblasted
Photo by artist

Cappy Thompson

EMPLOYING ICONOGRAPHY FROM A RANGE OF SOURCES, including Hindu and Buddhist philosophy, fables, and medieval legends, Cappy Thompson's work references a rich history of poetic narrative. Softly glowing and precisely detailed, the images she paints on her vessels seem to have been lifted from a book of children's tales. Thompson, who started out as a painter of stained glass, uses the transparency of her material to its fullest advantage. Her vessels are reverse-painted. She begins by sketching on the exterior of a form with a marking pen, then paints on the interior while working over a light table. She adds washes of black and colored vitreous enamels and fires each vessel four times—twice for the black layers and twice for colors.

As Thompson depicts them in her work, ordinary activities—a meal, a nap—become extraordinary, nearly ethereal. Colorful and ebullient, the Washington state artist's pieces have a timeless quality. Recognized as the foremost American practitioner of the art of transparent enameling, Thompson has been working with glass since 1976.

I Receive a Great Blessing from the Sun and the Moon: I Will Be an Artist and Walk the Path of Beauty | 1995 ▶

16 x 15½ x 15½ inches (40.6 x 39.4 x 39.4 cm)
Blown glass, vitreous enamels; reverse painted
Photo by Michael Seidl

◀ **The Kingdom Within** | 2001

28 x 14½ x 14½ inches
(71.1 x 36.8 x 36.8 cm)
Blown glass, vitreous enamels;
reverse painted

Photo by Russell Johnson

Dream Tapestry | 1999 ▶

15¾ x 13½ x 13½ inches
(40 x 34.3 x 34.3 cm)
Blown glass, vitreous enamels;
reverse painted

Photos by Michael Seidl

◀ **Lovers Dreaming a Dream** | 1996

16 x 16 x 16 inches (40.6 x 40.6 x 40.6 cm)
Blown glass, vitreous enamels; reverse painted

Photos by Michael Seidl

▼ **I Do Battle with My Evil "I"s on the Ground of Being** | 2000

19¼ x 14 x 14 inches (48.9 x 35.6 x 35.6 cm)
Blown glass, vitreous enamels; reverse painted

Photo by Russell Johnson

▼ **I Was Dreaming of Spirit Animals** | 1997

11½ x 16 x 16 inches (29.2 x 40.6 x 40.6 cm)
Blown glass, vitreous enamels; reverse painted

Photo by Michael Seidl

"My design process is intuitive. Sometimes it feels like the image is making itself, and everything simply unfolds. At other times, I feel like I'm carving the work out of stone—I only know that the image isn't right yet."

◀ **Perfect Life** | 1993
19½ x 15¾ x 15¾ inches (49.5 x 40 x 40 cm)
Blown glass, vitreous enamels; reverse painted
Photos by Michael Seidl

▼ **Family Portrait with Muse** | 1993
21¾ x 12 x 12 inches (55.2 x 30.5 x 30.5 cm)
Blown glass, vitreous enamels; reverse painted
Photo by Michael Seidl

▲ **Canis and Rider** | 1992

22½ x 13 x 13 inches (57.2 x 33 x 33 cm)
Blown glass, vitreous enamels; reverse painted
Photo by Michael Seidl

▲ **Krishna and Me** | 1993

17½ x 11½ x 11½ inches (44.5 x 29.2 x 29.2 cm)
Blown glass, vitreous enamels; reverse painted
Photo by Michael Seidl

"Self-exploration and self-expression are two of my greatest inspirations. I look inward to get a nuanced view of the spiritual and psychological issues in my own life, and I hope the pictorial narratives that result touch the viewer, too."

▼ The Fire God Agni Blesses Me for Purposes of Glass Making | 1994

17 x 13 x 13 inches (43.2 x 33 x 33 cm)

Blown glass, vitreous enamels; reverse painted

Photos by Claire Garoutte

"I love the way a painting looks when it's seen through glass. It's like looking at a genie in a bottle."

▼ **My Vivid Imagination: A Portrait of the Artist and Her Muses** | 1997

22 x 11½ x 11½ inches (55.9 x 29.2 x 29.2 cm)

Blown glass, vitreous enamels; reverse painted

Photos by Michael Seidl

Kathleen Mulcahy

LIKE CHILDREN'S TOPS AWAITING A BURST OF ENERGY to set them in motion, the glass spinners made by Oakdale, Pennsylvania, artist Kathleen Mulcahy are small, toy-like treasures aswirl with contrasting colors. Investigating how different hues move together or repel each other during the hot process, Mulcahy uses color as a painter would, and she has developed a complex palette. Her work often explores the nature of transformation. She does not shy away from women's issues, and the human body in all its complexity and fragility has provided her with much subject matter over the years.

In collaboration with her husband, artist Ron Desmett, Mulcahy has created vessels blown of clear glass that incorporate complex geometric elements. The pieces are sandblasted to highlight the overall design. Founders of the Pittsburgh Glass Center, a public-access glass studio in Pittsburgh, Pennsylvania, Mulcahy and Desmett are permanent artists-in-residence at the center. Whether she's working alone or as part of a team, Mulcahy never fails to highlight the beauty of her medium in pieces that engage the viewer on multiple levels.

Mulcahy has won many awards, including grants from the National Endowment for the Arts and the Fulbright Foundation, and her work is held in collections around the United States.

Golden Spinner Group | 2000 ▶
18 x 32 x 24 inches
(45.7 x 81.3 x 61 cm)
Blown glass
Photo by artist

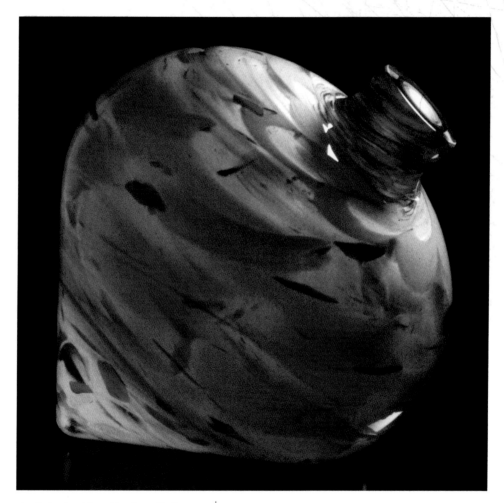

▲ **Appalachian Spring: Spinner** │ 2007
  16 x 17 x 20 inches (40.6 x 43.2 x 50.8 cm)
  Blown glass
  Photo by artist

Femme: Belle | 1994 ▶

50 x 8 x 30 inches
(127 x 20.3 x 76.2 cm)
Blown glass, mixed media;
sandblasted

Photo by artist

"My work usually alludes to the feminine, to questions about beauty and form. I'm challenged by the ways in which a form can be suspended and pared down to its essence."

◀ **In the Mood** │ 1989
    52 x 18 x 20 inches
    (132.1 x 45.7 x 50.8 cm)
    Blown glass, wood
    Photo by artist

◀ **Crossings: A Collaboration with Ron Desmett** | 1983

20 x 13 x 13 inches (50.8 x 33 x 33 cm)

Blown glass; sandblasted, cast

Photos by artist

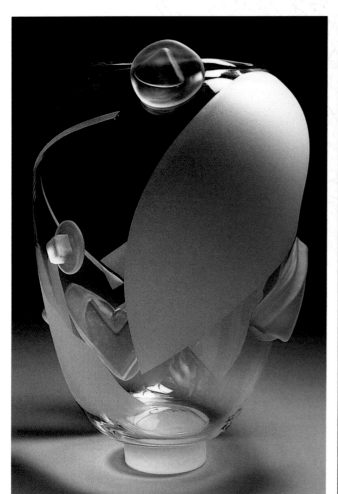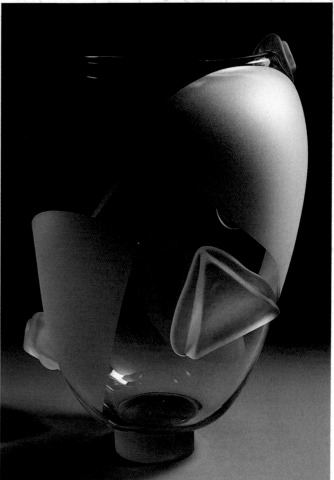

▲ **Crossings: A Collaboration with Ron Desmett** │ 1982

22 x 14 x 14 inches (55.9 x 35.6 x 35.6 cm)
Blown glass; sand blasted, cast additions
Photos by artist

"Glass has a wonderful surface. I love its ability to carry transparent and opaque elements—

bits that can collide, fuse, or intersect with others to create depth and intensity."

"I'm interested in the intrinsic gesture that creates, in the form, a frozen moment of off-balance movement—a motion like dropping or spinning that can lead to transformation."

▲ **Vapors: An Installation** | 1992

50 x 15 x 10 inches
(127 x 38.1 x 25.4 cm)
Blown glass, steel armatures;
acid etched

Photos by artist

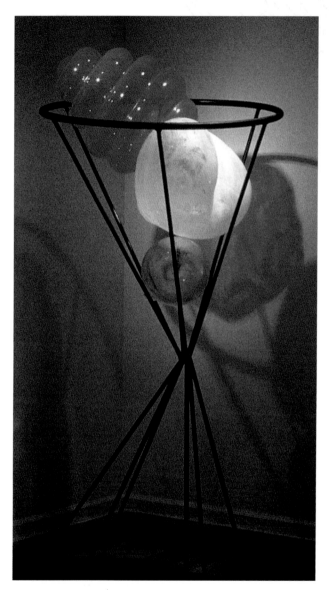

▲ **Double Top** | 1992

84 x 36 x 36 inches (213.4 x 91.4 x 91.4 cm)

Blown glass, steel

Photo by artist

▲ **FACE** | 2007

19 x 10 x 9 inches (48.3 x 25.4 x 22.9 cm)

Blown glass; etched

Photo by artist

Robert Carlson

CARLSON

MYTHOLOGY AND DREAM STATES ARE TOPICS that lie at the heart of Robert Carlson's vibrant, startling work. His vessels feature twisted, grotesque imagery—unsettling human forms that seem to come from a dream sequence. Carlson paints this imagery on oddly blown glass shapes that function more as three-dimensional canvases than as vessels. He uses the transparent nature of the glass to his advantage, letting it serve as a neutral background for multihued pictorials.

Carlson's figures—undulating, raw, complex, and sometimes plucked from popular culture—take viewers on an unforgettable journey. Exuding a quality of timelessness, his goblets seem like chalices ready to be filled with an otherworldly potion. They often feature imagery that has the frankness of a hallucination. Carlson's work—primitive yet sophisticated, simple yet calculating—haunts the imagination.

Carlson has been working with glass since 1981, and he lives in Washington state. His pieces are in collections around the world.

Odysseus | 1992 ▶
10 x 14 inches
(25.4 x 35.6 cm)
Blown glass, enamel paint,
gold leaf
Photo by Roger Schreiber

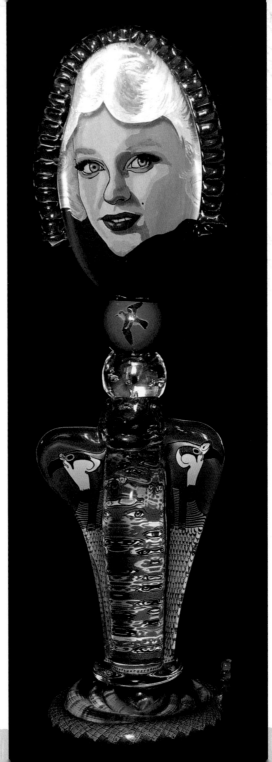

◀ Priestess | 2006

9 x 10 x 34 inches
(22.9 x 25.4 x 86.4 cm)
Blown glass, enamel paint,
adhesive

Photo by artist

▼ **Axis Mundi** | 1996

16 x 13 x 32 inches (40.6 x 33 x 81.3 cm)
Blown glass, wood, enamel paint, gold leaf,
copper leaf
Photo by Roger Schreiber

▲ **Janus** | 1995

18 x 13 x 21 inches (45.7 x 33 x 53.3 cm)
Blown glass, enamel paint, gold leaf, copper leaf,
fiberglass, mastic, grout, mirror
Photo by Roger Schreiber

"At heart I'm a three-dimensional artist, which is why I love using glass as my medium. Clear glass transmits images through itself, allowing me to turn an object composed of surfaces into an object with both surfaces and an interior."

▲ Hephaestus | 1994

17 x 10 x 9 inches
(43.2 x 25.4 x 22.9 cm)
Blown glass, enamel paint,
gold leaf

Photo by Roger Schreiber

▲ Jerusalem | 2001

10 x 18 x 21 inches (25.4 x 45.7 x 53.3 cm)
Blown plate glass, enamel paint, gold leaf, adhesive

Photo by Roger Schreiber

◀ **Lao Tsu's 82nd Poem** | 2006

43 x 12 inches (109.2 x 30.5 cm)
Blown glass, enamel paint,
adhesive

Photo by Robert Carlson

The Muse | 2000 ▶

8 x 8 x 37 inches
(20.3 x 20.3 x 94 cm)
Blown glass, enamel paint,
gold leaf, copper leaf

Photo by Roger Schreiber

ROBERT **CARLSON**

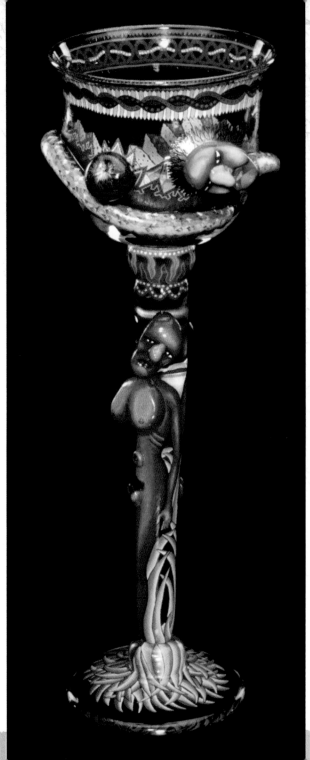

"My pieces have to be about more than just glass and its inherent properties. With paint I'm able to create narrative sculptures from this beautiful and seductive material."

Progeny | 1988 ▶

20 x 8 inches (50.8 x 20.3 cm)
Blown glass, enamel paint

Photo by Rob Vinnedge

ROBERT CARLSON

◀ **Pan** | 1990

8 x 25 inches
(20.3 x 63.5 cm)
Blown glass,
enamel paint

Photo by Rob Vinnedge

Apis Arcana | 1988 ▶

29 x 10 x 8 inches
(73.7 x 25.4 x 20.3 cm)
Blown glass,
enamel paint

Photo by Rob Vinnedge

"Glass gives my sculptures form.

Paint gives them meaning."

◀ **East of Eden** │ 2001

    33 x 14 x 10 inches
    (83.3 x 35.6 x 25.4 cm)
    Blown glass, enamel paint,
    gold leaf, copper leaf
    Photo by Roger Schreiber

ROBERT **CARLSON**

DONEFER

Laura Donefer

USING THE VESSEL AS A VEHICLE FOR ARTICULATING a range of thoughts and moods, Laura Donefer experiments with different modes of expression. Combining glass with earthy, natural materials that are personal to her worldview, she creates witchpots, vases, candleholders, and other heavily textured pieces. Donefer celebrates womanhood in her work, drawing on her female relationships for inspiration. From dull metallic surfaces to bright polished exteriors, her vessels exhibit a range of textures and reflect a bold aesthetic.

Whether exploring white in its various shades or setting up shocking combinations of hues, Donefer uses color to probe emotion, and she digs deep to create dramatic effects. Featuring ornate, decorative handles, her pots and baskets are meticulously finished with glass beads and found objects such as animal skulls, bones, hair, and feathers. As a result, Donefer's pieces possess a special spiritual quality. Primal and captivating, her unforgettable vessels are in a class by themselves.

Donefer, who lives in Harrowsmith, Ontario, in Canada, has work in numerous museums, including the Museum of Arts and Design in New York City and the Museo de Vidrio in Monterrey, Mexico.

Orange Dot Amulet Basket | 2007 ▶

29 x 22 x 20 inches (73.7 x 55.9 x 50.8 cm)
Blown glass, frit bits; sandblasted, torch worked
Photo by Stephen Wild

◄ Tangerine Bonnechance Basket │ 2009

20 x 11 x 10 inches (50.8 x 27.9 x 25.4 cm)
Blown glass; sandblasted

Photos by Stephen Wild

MASTERS: BLOWN GLASS

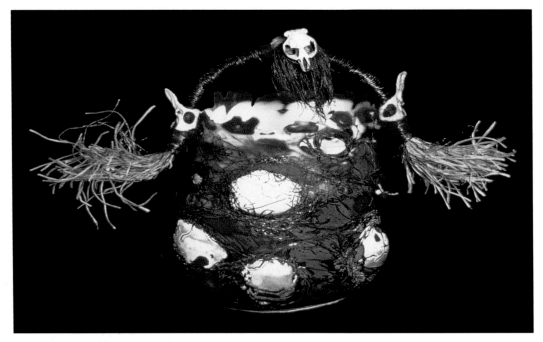

▲ **White Nest Witch Pot** | 1990

18 x 22 x 13 inches (45.7 x 55.9 x 76.2 cm)
Blown glass, copper, mixed media
Photo by David Hall

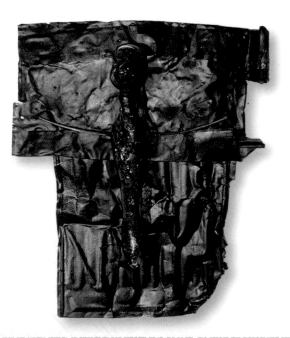

Resurrect (Triptych) | 2002 ▶

26 x 24 x 4 inches (66 x 61 x 10.2 cm)
Blown glass, copper, melon seeds,
heron bones, beaver teeth, found metal
Photo by Stephen Wild

"Glass is my metaphor for life. It can be totally transparent and reveal what's inside, or opaque and mysterious, providing only glimpses of what's hidden."

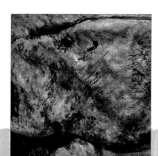

▲ **Wild Woods Witch Pot** | 2003

18 x 20 x 18 inches (45.7 x 50.8 x 45.7 cm)
Blown glass, mica-impregnated glass, antler,
skull, moss, copper; solid worked

Photos by Stephen Wild

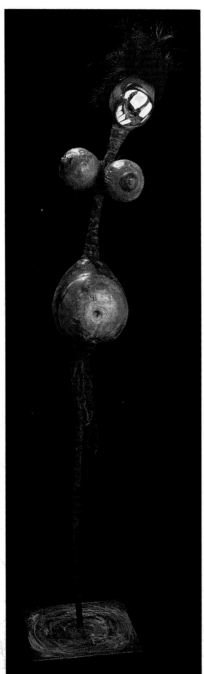

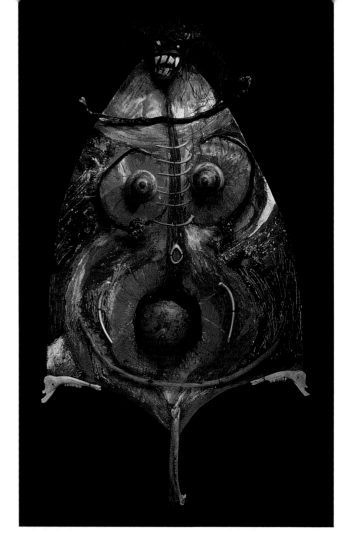

▲ **Kali-Black Mother Time** | 1987

  72 x 60 x 12 inches (182.9 x 152.4 x 30.5 cm)
  Blown glass, mixed media
  Photo by Peter Hogan

◀ **Core Series: Silent Scream** | 1988

  66 x 13 x 13 inches (33 x 33 x 167.6 cm)
  Blown glass, metal
  Photos by David Hall

"I celebrate life through fire."

▲ Bereft (Installation) | 2003

84 x 360 x 28 inches (213.4 x 914.4 x 71.1 cm)
Blown glass jars, found objects, beeswax, burlap; sealed

Photos by Stephen Wild

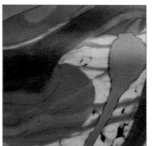

▲ **Spiral Amulet Baskets** | 2006

20 x 30 x 10 inches (50.8 x 76.2 x 25.4 cm)
Blown glass; torch worked

Photos by Stephen Wild

▼ **La Vida Loca Amulet Basket** | 2007

26 x 20 x 18 inches (66 x 50.8 x 45.7 cm)
Blown glass, turquoise, coral; torch worked

Photos by Stephen Wild

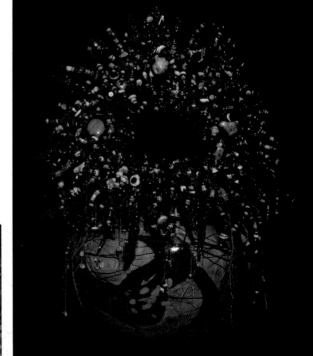

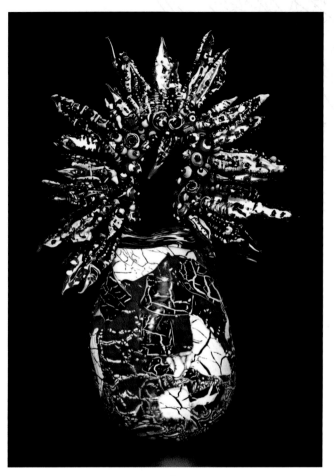

▲ **Afrique Amulet Basket** | 2007

 12 x 9 x 6 inches (30.5 x 22.9 x 15.2 cm)
 Blown glass; torch worked

 Photo by Stephen Wild

▲ **Winterpearl Bonnechance Basket** | 2009

 24 x 22 x 16 inches (61 x 55.9 x 40.6 cm)
 Blown glass, pearls; torch worked

 Photo by Stephen Wild

"There's a crazy, kamikaze quality to working with glass. It feels like all or nothing.**"**

William Bernstein

GLASS AS A PAINTED VESSEL TAKES MANY FORMS for Burnsville, North Carolina, artist William Bernstein. Having come to the medium as a potter in the 1960s, he still plays with traditional, utilitarian clay-pot forms, but now explores the quality of transparency that glass can bring to the pieces. He collaborates with Katherine Bernstein, his wife, on functional objects such as pitchers and tumblers, adding colorful, expressionistic caricatures to each work.

Using offbeat forms to enhance the humor of his pieces, Bernstein paints portraits on often whimsically shaped vessels. Just as a ceramist adds glazes to clay, he applies layers of vitreous enamels to his glass pieces, kiln-firing them after each application. For other pieces, he manipulates colored glass rods with a torch during the blowing process, a technique that gives each vessel slight textural relief. Bernstein brings to his innovative glass creations his sense of sophisticated wit and a deep understanding of human psychology. His work has been exhibited at the Museum of Arts and Design in New York City, The Hague in the Netherlands, and museums around the world.

◀ **Leaf Pitcher and Tumblers** │ 2005

Collaboration with Katherine Bernstein
Tumblers: 4½ x 3 x 3 inches
(11.4 x 7.6 x 7.6 cm) each
Pitcher: 9 x 7 x 5 inches
(22.9 x 17.8 x 12.7 cm)
Blown glass; hot cane drawing
Photo by Tom Mills

◀ **Self-Portrait with Interior** │ 2009

9½ x 7 x 7 inches
(24.1 x 17.8 x 17.8 cm)
Blown glass, vitreous enamels
Photo by Tom Mills

Tennis Situation | 2007 ▶

12 x 10 x 4 inches
(30.5 x 25.4 x 12.7 cm)
Blown glass, vitreous enamels

Photo by Tom Mills

"My work expresses an intense personal vision—one that's guided by a profound love of visual motion."

Face Goblet | 1999 ▶

Collaboration with Katherine Bernstein
8½ x 3½ x 3½ inches
(21.6 x 8.9 x 8.9 cm)
Blown glass; hot cane drawing
Photo by John Littleton

WILLIAM **BERNSTEIN**

"I enjoy drawing and painting on paper, and I think this often contributes to the way I approach glass."

▲ **Chickens** | 2008
Each: 9 x 8 x 5 inches (22.9 x 20.3 x 12.7 cm)
Blown and hot-tooled glass
Photo by Tom Mills

▼ Betty | 2005

10 x 5½ x 5½ inches (25.4 x 14 x 14 cm)
Blown glass; hot cane drawing
Photo by Tom Mills

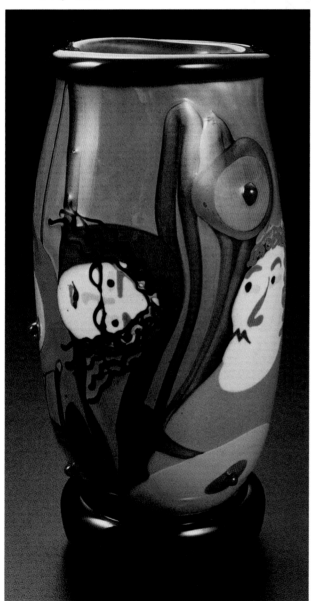

▼ Glassblower as Glass | 2004

17 x 12 x 8 inches (43.2 x 30.5 x 20.3 cm)
Blown glass; hot cane drawing
Photo by John Littleton

WILLIAM BERNSTEIN

◀ **Couple in the Tub** | 2009

10 x 7 x 7 inches (25.4 x 17.8 x 17.8 cm)
Blown glass, vitreous enamels
Photo by Tom Mills

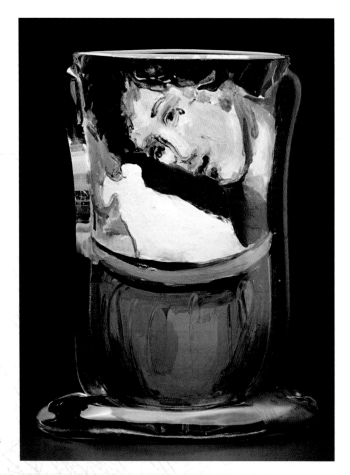

Bread Dough | 2008 ▶

9½ x 8 x 5 inches
(24.1 x 20.3 x 12.7 cm)
Blown glass, vitreous enamels
Photo by Tom Mills

"I'm drawn to glass because of its sensuous softness when hot, its speed and grace, its rich historical association with the vessel, and because of the sheer joy of glass working."

▼ Susan | 2005
19 x 11 x 11 inches
(48.3 x 27.9 x 27.9 cm)
Blown glass, vitreous enamels
Photo by Tom Mills

▼ Susan Looking Left | 2006
15 x 6 x 6 inches
(38.1 x 15.2 x 15.2 cm)
Blown glass, vitreous enamels
Photo by Tom Mills

▲ Tom | 2005
18 x 8 x 8 inches
(45.7 x 20.3 x 20.3 cm)
Blown glass, vitreous enamels
Photo by Tom Mills

WILLIAM BERNSTEIN

Robin Cass

EXPLORING THE WAYS IN WHICH PEOPLE EXPERIENCE the physical world and relate to one another, the innovative work of New York artist Robin Cass serves as a complex inquiry into human nature. Inspired by the natural sciences, history, early industrial forms, and mechanical gadgets, Cass makes innovative sculptural pieces that feature a variety of components besides glass—modern, edgy materials such as rubber, metal mesh, and lead that stand in fascinating contrast to her fluid forms.

Cass' sleek, bird-shaped perfume ampoules are modeled after classical Roman glass vessels. These translucent blown-glass birds are pierced or joined in various ways, then layered with a heavy patina of materials that cause alchemical reactions and corrosion. Through these pieces, she examines the subtle paradoxes of human relationships—the precariousness of connection and the tension that accompanies desire. Both physically and psychologically compelling, her pieces are wonderfully engaging. Cass exhibits her work internationally and has received grants from the New York Foundation for the Arts and the Glass and Ceramic Center of Seto, Japan.

Minor Indulgence | 2009 ▶
14 x 24 x 10 inches (35.6 x 61 x 25.4 cm)
Blown glass, steel; sculpted, etched, painted
Photo by artist

◀ **Minor Utopia** | 2009

30 x 20 x 8 inches
(76.2 x 50.8 x 20.3 cm)
Blown glass, steel; etched, painted

Photo by Elizabeth Lamark

▲ **Seto Lantern** | 2003
7 x 10 x 10 inches (17.8 x 25.4 x 25.4 cm)
Blown glass; flat cane technique
Photos by artist

"While I use a variety of materials in my sculptural work, glass is at the heart of each piece. I've been seduced by its ability to take on a wide range of forms, textures, and colors."

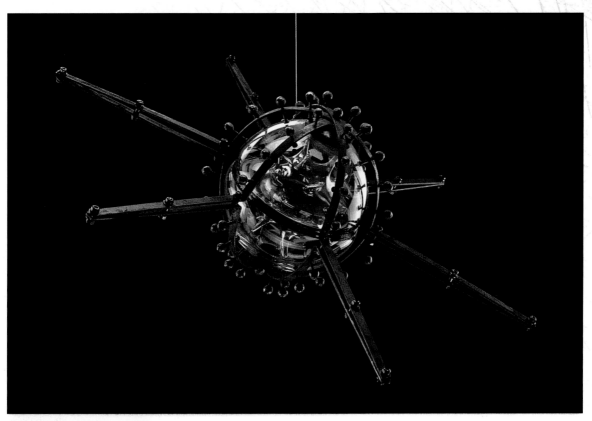

▲ **Diver III** | 2002

12 x 12 x 30 inches
(30.5 x 30.5 x 76.2 cm)
Blown glass, steel, rubber,
lead; silvered

Photos by Bruce Miller

"I want to elicit a number of associations and responses with each piece, on an intellectual as well as a visceral level. I try to raise questions and present possible realities for the viewer."

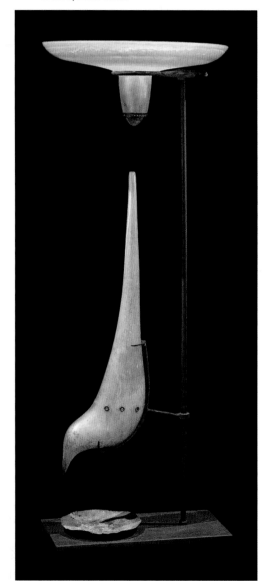

▼ Curative │ 2005
38 x 17 x 22 inches (96.5 x 43.2 x 55.9 cm)
Blown glass, steel, mixed media
Photo by Bruce Miller

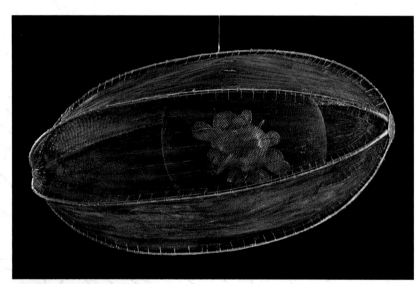

▲ Traveller III │ 2001
24 x 24 x 32 inches
(61 x 61 x 81.3 cm)
Blown glass, copper, brass mesh;
etched, painted
Photos by Bruce Miller

◀ **Trussed** │ 2005
 5 x 9 x 7 inches
 (12.7 x 22.9 x 17.8 cm)
 Blown glass, mixed media
 Photo by Bruce Miller

▲ **Abscess** │ 2006
 3 x 8 x 3½ inches (7.6 x 20.3 x 8.9 cm)
 Blown glass, felt, rubber, metal; painted
 Photo by Bruce Miller

"A fragile glass ampoule is a fitting metaphor for the human body and psyche. We humans are vulnerable containers, both literally and figuratively."

▲ **Fruition I** | 2006

38 x 18 x 25 inches
(96.5 x 45.7 x 63.5 cm)
Blown glass, copper;
flame worked, etched, painted
Photo by Elizabeth Lamark

Cleft | 2005 ▶

32 x 14 x 4 inches
(81.3 x 35.6 x 10.2 cm)
Blown glass; etched, painted
Photo by artist

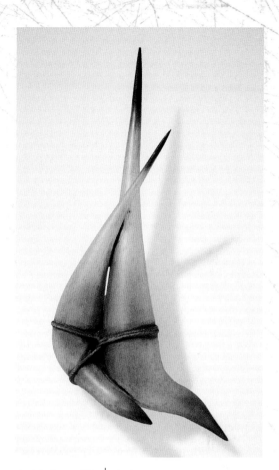

▲ **Linkage III** | 2006

22 x 9 x 4 inches (55.9 x 22.9 x 10.2 cm)
Blown glass, mixed media; etched, painted

Photo by Bill Klingensmith

◀ **Yield II** | 2006

34 x 14 x 8 inches (86.4 x 35.6 x 20.3 cm)
Blown glass, copper; flame worked,
painted, etched

Photo by Elizabeth Lamark

Richard Royal

WHIMSICAL YET FLUID, PLAYFUL YET SOPHISTICATED, Richard Royal's glass sculptures embrace a variety of attitudes and aesthetics. From large-scale creations—some more than four feet (1.2 m) tall—to intimate, decorative pieces, Royal's works consistently display a refined elegance. Royal combines curvaceous transparent and colored elements into assemblages that play off a carefully established sense of balance and symmetry. Some of his big vessels feature drapery-like pleats, which have been cut into layers of colored glass—layers that seem to undulate, instilling his work with movement and energy.

Possessing both a celebratory flare and a sense of carefully controlled decision-making, Royal's sculptures are organic, freeform structures that result from precise planning. Inspired by nature, some of his works—a blood-red capsule, for example, cracking open to send forth its seed—operate on a very primal level. In other pieces, Royal places brightly hued, solid sheets of glass along the outside of large-scale glass forms, setting up a dichotomy between interior and exterior that allows him to explore themes of personal development. The Seattle-based Royal was the first artist-in-residence at the Waterford Crystal Factory in Waterford, Ireland, in 1998. His work is included in the permanent collections of the Mint Museum of Art and Crafts in Charlotte, North Carolina, the High Museum of Art in Atlanta, Georgia, and the Daiichi Museum in Nagoya, Japan.

Pod Series | 2008 ▶
9 x 48 x 10 inches
(22.9 x 121.9 x 25.4 cm)
Hot sculpted glass,
blown glass
Photo by artist

Diamond Cut Series | 2009 ▶

42 x 13 x 9 inches
(106.7 x 33 x 22.9 cm)
Hot sculpted glass, blown glass
Photo by artist

◄ **Diamond Cut Series** | 2008

42 x 13 x 9 inches (106.7 x 33 x 22.9 cm)

Hot sculpted glass, blown glass

Photo by artist

Diamond Cut Series | 2005 ▶

36 x 13 x 11 inches (91.4 x 33 x 27.9 cm)

Hot sculpted glass, blown glass

Photo by artist

"After an earthquake in 2001, I had a bunch of broken pieces in my studio and was attracted to some of the remnants. They were very organic and primal in their deconstruction, and I found them inspiring. They seemed to represent a continuation of the process of making blown objects that I hadn't explored."

▲ **Shelter Series** │ 2001

  Largest: 43 x 8 x 9 inches (109.2 x 20.3 x 22.9 cm)
  Hot sculpted glass
  Photo by artist

Optical Lens Series │ 2006 ▶

  24 x 18 inches (61 x 45.7 cm)
  Blown glass
  Photo by artist

RICHARD ROYAL

◀ **Charisma** │ 2004

47 x 9 x 8 inches
(119.4 x 22.9 x 20.3 cm)
Blown glass, metal stand

Photo by artist

Fleur │ 2009 ▶

54 x 24 x 11 inches
(137.2 x 61 x 27.9 cm)
Hot sculpted glass,
blown glass

Photo by artist

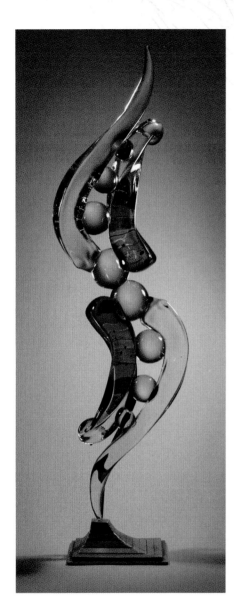

Cirque | 2008 ▶

48 x 12 x 9 inches
(121.9 x 30.5 x 22.9 cm)
Hot sculpted glass,
graphic metal stand

Photo by artist

◀ **Trail** | 2008

51 x 13 x 9 inches
(129.5 x 33 x 22.9 cm)
Hot sculpted glass, clear glass,
graphic metal stand

Photo by artist

"Some of my works serve as metaphors for self-exploration. I create pieces that represent the outer self, and I try to indicate, through the decorative process, ways of exploring the inner self."

"I'm fascinated by the theory that all things have a geometric significance—that if you break something down, eventually you'll find a geometric structure in its essence. To portray this concept in my work, I create organic sculptures using rigid components."

▲ Golden Earth, Tourmaline Sky | 2008
34 x 34 x 11 inches (86.4 x 86.4 x 27.9 cm)
Mold-blown glass, hot sculpted glass
Photo by artist

▲ **Red Star** | 2008

38 x 36 x 36 inches (96.5 x 91.4 x 91.4 cm)
Mold-blown glass, hot sculpted glass, metal stand

Photo by artist

Paul Marioni

FASCINATED BY THE KINETIC POSSIBILITIES of glass sculpture, Paul Marioni creates playful work that he wants viewers to touch. His pieces are often slumped, so that they rock to and fro—movement that produces magical effects with light as it moves through the glass. Irreverent and bold, these interactive works defy glass' reputation as a fragile and delicate medium.

Marioni's painted vessels have a sharpened perspective—one that embraces the concerns and conflicts that so frequently define our lives. Characterized by intelligence, insight, and a confident discernment of human nature, these works feature human figures, including the occasional self-portrait, and are rendered with a bemused sense of endearment. The sensuality of sleek provocative forms shines through in his other works—vessels inspired by the human body provide ample of evidence of Marioni's whimsical sense of humor.

One of the founding members of the American studio glass movement and a winner of the Glass Art Society's Lifetime Achievement Award, Marioni has taught throughout the United States. His work has been shown internationally, with exhibits at the Smithsonian Institution in Washington, D.C., the Corning Museum in Corning, New York, and the Glasmuseum in Frauenau, Germany. He lives in Seattle, Washington.

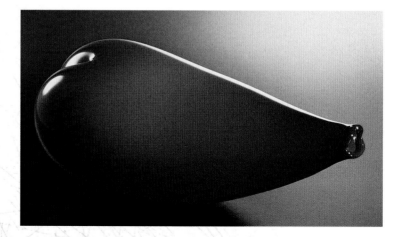

Whistling Vase (Kinetic) | 2001 ▶
6 x 15 x 6 inches (15.2 x 38.1 x 15.2 cm)
Blown glass
Photo by Russell Johnson

▲ **Spirits Lifting** | 2005

9 x 10 x 4 inches (22.9 x 25.4 x 10.2 cm)

Blown glass, paint

Photo by Russell Johnson

▲ **Me and My Guardian Angel** | 2006

    9 x 10 x 5 inches (22.9 x 25.4 x 12.7 cm)

    Blown glass, paint

    Photo by Russell Johnson

"The penetration of the momentary by the eternal and the potential for dreams to bring unconscious material to our awareness are two of the forces that drive my work."

Frida Kahlo | 1992 ▶

    26 x 9 x 9 inches (66 x 22.9 x 22.9 cm)

    Blown glass, paint

    Photo by Roger Schreiber

14 x 6 x 6 inches (35.6 x 15.2 x 15.2 cm)
Blown glass, paint
Photo by Roger Schreiber

▲ **Hot Nights** │ 1987

14 x 7 x 7 inches (35.6 x 17.8 x 17.8 cm)
Blown glass, paint
Photo by Roger Schreiber

PAUL **MARIONI**

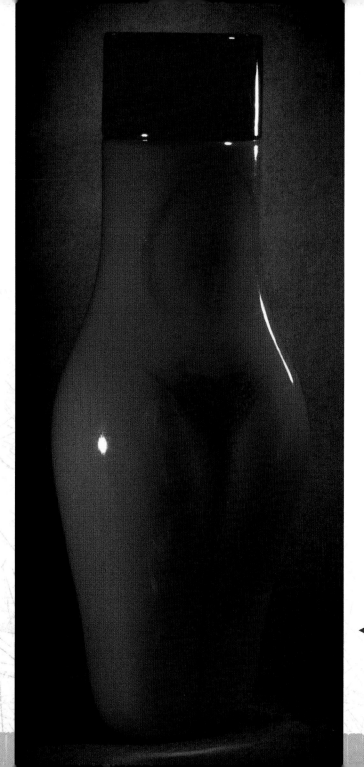

"My work is often

purposefully left open to

interpretation.

I don't want to tell

viewers what to think;

I want to make

them think."

◀ **Eve** │ 1993

21 x 8 x 6 inches (53.3 x 20.3 x 15.2 cm)

Blown glass, paint

Photo by Roger Schreiber

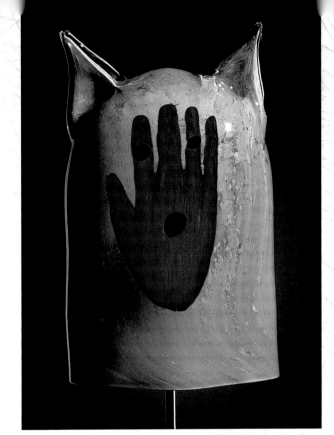

▲ **Fire Mask** | 2000

21 x 10 x 6 inches (53.3 x 25.4 x 15.2 cm)
Blown glass, paint
Photo by Russell Johnson

◀ **Adam** | 1993

21 x 8 x 6 inches (53.3 x 20.3 x 15.2 cm)
Blown glass, paint
Photo by Roger Schreiber

PAUL MARIONI

▲ **The Something or Other Society** | 2006

　11 x 6 x 6 inches (27.6 x 15.2 x 15.2 cm)
　Blown glass, paint
　Photo by Russell Johnson

▲ **The Man Who Loved Only Numbers** | 2006

　14 x 10 x 5 inches (35.6 x 25.4 x 12.7 cm)
　Blown glass, paint
　Photo by Russell Johnson

"I have a surrealist's attitude. I work with glass because it can be used to manipulate light and create illusions of motion or three-dimensionality."

◄ Watching | 2009
9 x 5 x 5 inches
(22.9 x 12.7 x 12.7 cm)
Blown glass, paint
Photos by Russell Johnson

PAUL MARIONI

327

About the Curator

Susan M. Rossi-Wilcox is the editor of *Journal of the Glass Art Society* and a recipient of the Corning Museum of Glass' Rakow Research Fellowship. Before retiring from Harvard University in 2007, she served as Curatorial Associate at the university's Botanical Museum and as administrator of its Glass Flowers collection. Rossi-Wilcox has curated several exhibitions on glass and lectured extensively. She is the author of *Dinner for Dickens: The Culinary History of Mrs. Charles Dickens' Menu Books* (2005) and *Drawing upon Nature: Studies for the Blaschkas' Glass Models*, co-authored with David Whitehouse (2007). She reviews books for *Journal of Popular Culture* and served on the Board of Directors of the Glass Art Society.

Acknowledgments

Susan Rossi-Wilcox curated this remarkable collection with passion and care. Susan is an outstanding, committed ambassador for the glass-art community. Shane Fero, president of the Glass Art Society, offered enthusiastic support in the development of this project. Production editor Julie Hale led a fine editorial team in bringing the many elements of the book together effectively, assisted by Larry Shea, Dawn Dillingham, Meagan Shirlen, Kathy Sheldon, and Wolf Hoelscher. In art design and layout, Kay Holmes Stafford, Megan Kirby, Jeff Hamilton, and Shannon Yokeley all did excellent work, executing a terrific series design by Kristi Pfeffer. Lark Books' Craft Your Life team leader Nicole McConville and senior art director Chris Bryant provided valuable direction.

Most of all, I want to thank the master glassworkers who participated by submitting commentary and images of their pieces. Blown glass is an exciting, growing medium, and this collection of their beautiful work is a testament to the range, vibrancy, and inventiveness of the glass art being produced today.

Ray Hemachandra, senior editor

Portrait Photographers

Thank you to the photographers whose portraits of the artists appear in this book:

Gabriella Bisetto, photo by Mark Thompson

Sonja Blomdahl, photo by Ray Weiss

Robin Cass, photo by Bill Kingensmith

Scott Chaseling, photo by Paul Louis

Dan Dailey, photo by Russell Johnson

Laura Donefer, photo by Suzy Lamont

Benjamin Edols and Kathy Elliott, photo by Keith Saunders

Peter Houk, photo by Rosemarie Marsh

Marvin Lipofsky, photo by Jeanette Bokhour

Richard Meitner, photo by Ron Zijlstra

Benjamin P. Moore, photo by Russell Johnson

Michael Rogers, photo by Bette Rogers

Dick Weiss, photo by Alex Otto

The photos of William Bernstein, Jane Bruce, Robert Carlson, Wendy J. Fairclough, Katherine Gray, William Gudenrath, Brian Hirst, Joey Kirkpatrick, Flora Mace, Dante Marioni, Paul Marioni, Richard Marquis, Mark Matthews, Debora Moore, William Morris, Nick Mount, Kathleen Mulcahy, Joel Philip Myers, Kait Rhoads, Richard Royal, Josh Simpson, Preston Singletary, Daniel Spitzer, Boyd Sugiki, Cappy Thompson, Sunny Wang, Maureen Williams, and Hiroshi Yamano are self-portraits.

Index of Artists